Wicca Magic Volume 1
Introduction To Candle Magic

Table of Contents

Introduction 1

Chapter 1: Wiccan Magic 4

Chapter 2: The Classical Elements And Spirit 31

Chapter 3: Wiccan Candle Magic 63

Chapter 4: Cleansing Your Candles 80

Chapter 5: Charging Your Candles 90

Chapter 6: Symbols For Your Candles 94

Chapter 7: Anointing Your Candles 98

Chapter 8: Candles And Love Spells 103

Chapter 9: Candles And Money Spells 116

Chapter 10: Candles And Healing Spells 119

Conclusion 122

Introduction

Thank you for purchasing this book! *Wicca Magic Volume 1: Introduction to Candle Magic* is designed to be a good starting point for people who are new to magic practices or to Wicca in general. Wicca is a relatively new pagan religious movement that was initially developed during the early- to the mid- 20th century and introduced to the public in the mid-20th century. Wicca draws from a large number of different pagan themes and practices, especially with regard to its theology and structure as a religion. However, Wicca has changed and evolved over time in order to take a large number of different forms and shapes. Because of the ways that Wicca has changed over time, there is no real official set of rules about the specifics of the practice of Wicca or the ways that those who practice are supposed to think or view their experiences or life. Wicca can be an incredibly varied and equally subjective practice, because of the uncertain history that it carries with it. Still, though, there are some particular elements of the Wicca that have stayed mostly consistent throughout the years, and this book will outline a number of those elements in order to help you learn about and how to practice effective and practical candle magic, as well as how to use it responsibly.

The concepts and practices of magic do not belong to any specific religious or spiritual tradition. There are many different cultures that have developed their own magical practices throughout the world. Magic can be practiced by any person of any religious background or set of beliefs. Wiccan practices and traditions, specifically, most magical practices are based on the practices of the folk healers from Europe, as well as the ancient Hermetic philosophies that were rediscovered during the Renaissance. But while there are a number of different spells and methods that have been passed down over the generations, the magic practices in Wicca is not typically considered to be a static art. There are new and different spells and approaches to those spells to help manifest the magical energies that are being developed and realized constantly. People who are willing to experiment with their magical practices are always finding new ways of doing so, and of using the various natural energies that make up the world and the various elements that exist within it.

Candles have a lot of different qualities that can be used to represent the way the elements work, but they can also vary in color as well. The colors of different objects, and especially candles, can be used for different effects based on the color of the candle. Certain colors are commonly associated with different forces or qualities, like luck, love, wealth, and even by death. There are certain colors that are very directly apparent, like the color red, which has always seemed to be associated with things like love and passion and even anger, in certain specific contexts. The color green is also commonly associated with things like abundance and growth, like the colors of the earth and the plants that grow within it. A candle can also be a very effective and balanced symbol or representation of the elements. Of course, this includes fire, but also the other three elements as well. The wick and the base of a candle are effective representations of the element of earth, as they are both made up of different aspects of the literal element of earth, as well as the ways that they are able to keep the flame grounded and support it as well. The wax can be an effective representation of the element of water, as it also transforms from a solid to a liquid, and then becomes a gas, in the same way, that water does when it is exposed to heat and can be a symbol of the shifting and changing nature of the element of water. The element of air is represented by the oxygen that keeps the flame alive, as well as the smoke that comes from the burning wick and the wax as the earth and water separate to temporarily become a part of the air. Of course, the flame itself is an aspect of the element of fire, being a literal flame. The spirit is even represented in candle magic when you charge the candle with your intention and action to send that magical energy off into the world.

Because of the strong connections that candles can have to the four classical elements, they can serve as extremely effective ways to strengthen a person's connection to those elements, which can make magic spells and rituals very simple and easy to understand or perform.

Chapter 1: Wiccan Magic

This book will be about Wiccan magic and how to use it effectively and responsibly. Wicca is a relatively new pagan religious movement that was initially developed during the early- to the mid- 20th century and introduced to the public in the mid-20th century. Wicca draws from a large number of different pagan themes and practices, especially with regards to its theology and structure as a religion. However, Wicca has changed and evolved over time in order to take a large number of different forms and shapes. Because of the ways that Wicca has changed over time, there is no real official set of rules about the specifics of the practice of Wicca or the ways that those who practice are supposed to think or view their experiences or life. Wicca can be an incredibly varied and equally subjective practice, because of the uncertain history that it carries with it. Still, though, there are some particular elements of the Wicca that have stayed mostly consistent in all or at least almost all of the different versions and iterations of the Wiccan beliefs and practices.

One of these elements that have been able to stay relatively consistent within the Wiccan belief system is the deities that Wicca and the people who practice Wicca revere. Typically, these deities have taken consistent, or at least similar, roles and forms. These forms are the God and the Goddess.

This pairing of the god and the goddess is one of the most iconic and easy to understand aspects of Wicca, especially when it is compared to a large number of other religions that have become popular over the years. The equal sense of emphasis on the masculine and feminine aspects of the world is a very important aspect of the Wiccan belief system and Wiccan practices. This dichotomy between these two genders and the ways that they can affect and can also be affected by the world both makeup two equally important aspects of Wicca. A lot of different groups or circles, or even individual people who practice Wicca might have different names that they use to refer to these two deities, but the deities' names are usually somewhat hidden or regarded as secret, so they will typically be referred to as simply "the God" and "the Goddess," when they are being discussed.

The God and the Goddess are a male and a female representation of the essences of the forces of life and creation that are responsible for all of the beings and objects in the world, and the laws that they follow, even including the cycles of life and death that all beings and entities on the earth must follow. As the supreme central deities of Wicca, the God and the Goddess are typically honored at the altar during every ritual that Wiccan practitioners perform, and even during the magical work that they perform as well. A large number of ancient cultures worshipped entities like these ones, representing both masculine and feminine aspects of the world, such as life and death or the earth and the sky. These deities typically represented opposing but equal and balanced forces that exist within the world, in some form or another. The modern Wiccan practice tries to emulate and adopt these beliefs of opposing, yet equal and balanced forces to some degree, which can clearly be seen in the prime deities of the Wiccan belief system, which are the God and the Goddess. And just as with other deities of these types, and belief systems that are built upon them, Wiccan beliefs also maintain that these deities form two "halves" of our world and their union is the event that created and sustains all of the life and creation in our world.

The pair of the God and the Goddess represents the different and opposing masculine and feminine energies that exist within the world. These energies or forces can be compared to a number of different concepts from various different cultures like the earth and the sea or sky, light and dark, life and death, or yin and yang, among a number of other kinds of forces, and can manifest in a number of different kinds of forms, like as humanoids, elements, or even simply as the forces of nature that they represent within nature. The god and the Goddess, to some people, might be viewed as manifestations and representations of the relationship that Wicca shares with the pagan religions that existed in western Europe before its adoption of Christianity and the Judeo-Christian beliefs that are much more common today.

The person who is commonly considered to have been the founder of the modern Wiccan belief system based his own "coven" around the idea and worship of a "Horned God" and the "Mother Goddess," which were his own representations of two archetypes that were very common in the pantheons that could be found in ancient European cultures, particularly the Celtic, Greek, and Norse cultures, and Egyptian civilizations. Two fairly well-known examples of these archetypes are a God that was called "Cernunnos," who was a Celtic god of fertility, life, and wealth, and who was commonly depicted to have had horns and the Greek Goddess of the Earth, who was a representation of the concept of motherhood. As two primary, universal deities, the masculine and female gods that are commonly accepted as part of the Wiccan belief system, the God and Goddess, are commonly understood to encompass each of these common individual aspects in order to allow for the Wiccan belief system to be compatible with the deities that were common in these ancient civilizations, and those deities can still be acknowledged and worshipped by many of today's Wiccans.

Most Wiccans, especially traditionalist ones, will typically view the individual gods and goddesses of these pantheons as "lesser" aspects or representations of the Wiccan God and Goddess, who maintain their status of Wicca's "Supreme" or "primary" deities. However, there are still some more eclectic practitioners of Wicca who do not recognize a strict hierarchy, and may even be a little bit more polytheistic in their beliefs, which means that for these people, the individual deities still maintain their own original positions in their pantheons, in addition to the Wiccan concepts of the God and Goddess. People who believe in this polytheistic structure will typically believe in another pantheon of deities, while also holding the Wiccan God and Goddess as their own deities separate from that pantheon or pantheons, or even as representations of various concepts or entities within those pantheons. Whatever an individual person's belief system may be, or their relationship with any ancient deities or religions, most Wiccans typically share a number of core beliefs, concepts, and traditions centered around the Wiccan God and Goddess.

The first of these primary, central deities that exist within most of the belief systems that Wiccan practitioners typically carry is the "God." As the more masculine part of the pair, God makes up half of the all-encompassing force of life that exists within common Wiccan beliefs, and the God is normally represented as being connected to and associated with aspects of or as a direct manifestation of the sun or as the "horned animals of the forest." The Wiccan God will sometimes take the role of the "God of the Hunt." When the God assumes this guise, he is commonly depicted as a man, wearing a headdress with horns or antlers, or even sometimes he might literally have the head of a stag or a goat, instead of the headdress. In this role, he performs two duties that go hand-in-hand, in assisting humans in finding sustenance in order to maintain their survival, as well as simultaneously protecting the animals and various creatures of the wild, maintaining a careful balance between the two in order to ensure that balance is kept among the life that exists within the world. In some of the earliest forms of the Wiccan religion, the "Horned God" also had strong connections to the concept of fertility, which can still be observed in some traditions that exist within modern circles of Wiccans. In addition to the Celtic god Cernunnos, the Horned god can also be connected to the Greek god called pan, who also performed a similar role, as well as welsh god "Bran," and an English figure named "Herne," as well as many others, including a figure called the "Green Man," who represents a very old, ancient archetype that can be found in stories from around the world, and who is most commonly depicted as simply a green man with a face that is either made of or surrounded by vines, leaves, or other kinds of plant life.

The other source of inspiration that the Wiccan God seems to be connected to is the Sun. A common trope that exists in many religious belief systems and pantheons is the masculine sun god being opposed and matched with the feminine moon goddess. The strong, warm light of the sun is commonly considered to be an aspect of male energy, and a very significant source of life and the growth and development of all different forms of life. As was briefly mentioned before, there are a large number of different ancient cultures that worshipped a "Sky Father," a god who maintained a connection with the sky or with the sun in one form or another, which is emulated and replicated to a certain degree by common modern Wiccan practices. The concept of the Wiccan Wheel of the Year also revolves around the cyclical relationship that is maintained by God, being connected to the sun, and the Goddess, representing the earth. In this model, the God will continually die off each year during the autumn season, staying dormant during the colder winter seasons, and will then also be "revived" or reborn in the spring, reaching his peak during the summer, when the warmth of the sun can be felt the most, or is at its strongest point, only to grow weak and "die" again in the fall. This cycle serves to parallel the cycle of the seasons and the cycles of growth that most plant life follows. A few common deities that will typically be representative of the "Sun God" are the Celtic god Lugh, the Egyptian God Ra, and the Greek God Apollo.

Within some particular Wiccan traditions, the wheel of the year and its connection to God is separated into two halves, as well. Instead of the Sun God simply dying off in the fall and winter, the wheel of the year dictates periods of time during which God will take different forms to change with the seasons. These forms are typically referred to as the "Oak King" and the "Holly King." These different forms are representative of the waxing and waning nature of the sun and its position to us throughout the year and as the seasons change. The Oak King and the Holly King will take turns ruling over life throughout the year as the other becomes weaker or "dies off" during its "off seasons." The Oak King will become stronger and will take up his reign during the "light half" of the year, which takes place during the spring and summer seasons, while the "dark half" of the year, which takes place during the autumn and the winter seasons, will give rise to the "Holly King," who will then "die-off" during the spring and the summer. The Oak King is, of course, named for the Oaktree, with its bright and decorative leaves, which symbolize the warmth and brightness of the seasons that he rules over. The Holly King, on the other hand, as the ruler of the "dark half" of the year, is named for the Holly tree, a cheery evergreen tree with its deep green leaves and bright red berries, which symbolize the much colder and harsher fall and winter seasons in the same way that the Oak symbolizes the spring and summer. Both of these trees are typically considered to be "sacred" to many Wiccans, witches, and other pagan practitioners, and both have also been treasured for the magical properties that they carry.

The Oak and Holly Kings are generally considered to be brothers and rivals, battling each other throughout the year and conquering each other as the seasons shift and they grow stronger and weaker at an inversed and opposite pace with the seasons. The dates that these battles are each won will depend on the tradition that is followed within specific circles, but usually will fall on the Solstices, with the Oak King taking control at the Winter Solstice, and the Holly king taking over and coming up on the Summer Solstice, since these dates (or sabbats) are the official markers to signify the waxing and waning of the sun in relation to the earth. However, there are many other traditions, which consider this change to take place during the Equinoxes of Spring and Autumn, which will have the Holly King reach the height of his power during the Winter Solstice, when the "dark season" reaches its peak, and the Oak king reaching his peak during the Summer Solstice, when the light is the strongest. Many people believe that this alternative version makes a little bit more sense in terms of the ways that the seasons are generally experiences. However, both of these interpretations of the wheel of the year and the nature of the Oak King and the Holly King serve to highlight the nature of the wheel of the year in similar ways. The primary theme of this concept and the ways that the oak and holly kings work, and the passage and transitions of the seasons as well as the simple passage of time.

Some Wiccans in certain circles even tend to see the Oak King and the Holly King as twinned aspects and halves of the whole that makes up the Wiccan concept of the God in a constant and eternal battle with each other to gain the love and the attention of their Goddess. Many people don't see the two kings in the same way, but instead, consider this legend of the two kings as simply another layer of the larger concept of the wheel of the year. The true origin of the story of the Oak King and the Holly King is mostly unknown, so it is difficult to guess at the original intent of the story, but regardless, they have become a very important aspect of the lore that is involved in many different variations of pagan and Wiccan traditions. Although the concept of the Oak and Holly kings is not exclusive to Wiccan practices, they do very clearly fit in with the lore and the beliefs that are carried by many Wiccan practitioners, especially with their focus on opposing forces, like light and dark, and various cycles of life and death in a number of different forms. These concepts and the combination of the cycle of life and death with the opposing forces that are present in Wiccan traditions are very likely the origins of a lot of the stories and lore that exist within those traditions and help to explain that balance is necessary for all aspects of life. There can be no light without the dark, and the two forces have to find a balance in order to coexist properly.

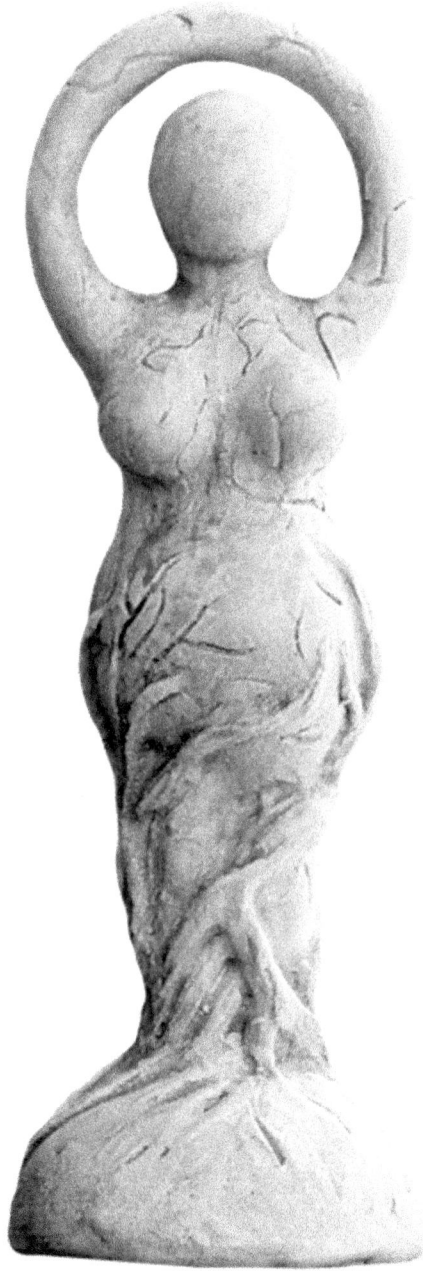

As the feminine half of this all-encompassing life force, the Goddess is associated with both the Earth and the Moon. In her association with the Moon, the Wiccan Goddess rules the night and the ocean tides as well as the reproductive cycles of women and the realm of the human psyche. In many Wiccan traditions, the Goddess takes a three-fold form known as the Triple Goddess. Her individual aspects known as the Maiden, the Mother, and the Crone are aligned with the phases of the Moon's cycle as it orbits the Earth—waxing, Full, and waning. In this watery element, the Goddess is associated with emotion, intuition, and the wisdom that comes from engaging with our shadow side.

The other deity that exists within most Wiccan traditions is the Goddess. The goddess commonly represents the earth and the moon. The Wiccan goddess, as she is associated with the moon, is the ruler of the night. She controls the oceans and the tides as well as the reproductive cycles of a woman and the human psyche. In a lot of different Wiccan traditions, the goddess will take three different forms, which make up three parts of what is commonly referred to as the "triple goddess." The three aspects of this form are known commonly as the maiden, the mother, and the crone, and each of these forms aligns themselves with the different places of the cycle of the moon. These are the Waxing, waning, and full moons, and each represents a different stage of life. If the Sun god represents the cycle of life and death, the moon goddess is representative of everything that happens between the points of birth and death. The Goddess is also very commonly associated with the concepts of emotion, intuition, and wisdom, particularly as it relates to the experience that we gain throughout life.

The goddess is also connected to the earth as well. Like the earth, the goddess is representative of the physical energy that can allow life to bind itself to, allowing life to grow and flourish. She is associated with domesticated animals, fields, and crops, and the growth and development that they experience throughout their life cycles. She plays the roles of the mother to all of the beings and entities that exist within and on the earth, as well as the partner of the god, and their individual cycles make up the forces that allow for the existence of all life on earth and the rules that they follow regarding their birth, life, and death as time progresses and the seasons change. Their cycles of life and death allow the wheel of the year to continue to turn and clear away old things to allow for the new to take over in an eternal cycle of life and death.

As the feminine aspect of the pair that makes up all of the forces of life and creation that exist in the world, and as has been mentioned before, the goddess is commonly associated with both the earth and the moon. As the representation of the earth, the goddess represents the grounded physical energy that tethers all life on earth to herself and allows that life to grow and flourish. Her energy is typically seen as more nurturing and tender, and is flexible and pliable, keeping in line with the fact that she essentially represents growth and change. As the partner to the God, the Goddess symbolizes the cycles of growth and change, and those forces combine with the God's more rigid nature and his cycles of life and death in order to maintain the "turning" of the wheel of the year, which allow for the passage of time and the clearing away of the old in exchange for the introduction of new things. The Wiccan Goddess, as connected to the earth, is commonly associated with the Greek Goddess Gaia, as well as the Celtic goddess Brighid and the Egyptian Goddess Isis.

The Goddess is also commonly associated with the moon, and in this context, it is connected to the reproductive cycles of women as well as the human psyche. In this connection with the moon, she also has control over the oceans and the tides, as well as the concepts of emotion and intuition. If the Wiccan God and his orientation toward direct action can be compared to the concept of "yang" energy, then the Goddess would represent his other half, and be compared to the concept of "yin," combining to make up the push and pull of the yin and yang. The Goddess, in this context of her connection with the moon, also draws some parallels to other deities from other cultures, such as Artemis, the Greek Goddess, as well as the Celtic Goddess Cerridwen and the Roman goddess Diana.

The Wiccan Goddess is connected with the moon in a slightly different way to the way that the god is connected with the sun, however, because of the slightly different relationship that the moon has with the earth. The moon is much closer to the earth than the sun is and it has its own unique cycle that moves at a slightly quicker pace than the sun. This is the origin of the concept of the "triple goddess" that was mentioned earlier, as well. The goddess, in this divided sense, is a deity with three distinct forms, each with their own individual and unique aspects that each represent the moon. These three forms are referred to as the maiden, the mother, and the crone, with each of these forms representing a phase in the lunar cycle, as well as different stages in the lives of women before, during, and after their body is able to produce life. However, the triple goddess is a little bit more complicated than that. While women will generally progress in a linear fashion through these three phases of the goddess' forms in a literal sense over the course of her life, each aspect of the triple goddess also has various qualities that can relate to every person at various times in their lives, whether they are male or female, and regardless of the current stage of life that they are in. The triple goddess is also thought to be a reflection of the complex nature of the human psyche, and is also representative of the inherent cycles of life and death that all living beings that exist on the earth experience, even within the literal span of their lifetimes, in the sense that life evolves and changes as time goes on. Over time, people or animals will shed their skin, shells, or fur. They will grow and experience new things that change how they react to certain events and they will develop relationships with other people or animals who also have natures just as complex as their own. The concept of the triple goddess reflects those aspects of life very effectively and can be applied to everything and everyone, regardless of sex or gender, or their current age.

The actual concept of the triple deity can be traced back to the Celtic goddess Brighid, who was thought to rule over three separate, but vital skills within the Celtic society, which were healing, poetry, and smithcraft. Another example of this type of deity is the Greek goddess Hera, who also had three separate roles, which were very similar to the three phases of the Wiccan triple goddess: Girl, woman, and widow.

However, instead of being a single entity that takes three separate forms, like with the case of Hera and Brighid, the Wiccan Triple Goddess is usually represented as being three separate entities, each making up their own aspect of the concept of the Wiccan goddess as a whole, in a similar way to how the Oak King and the Holly kind each represent two parts of the whole Wiccan god. Each aspect of the triple goddess is also related to their own concepts, such as particular seasons, natural phenomena, and even human characteristics and aspects of life that exists on earth. These different associations can be used to call on the aspect of the goddess that is the most appropriate during things like magical work, worship, rituals, or prayers.

The first aspect that will be discussed here is the Maiden. The maiden aligns with the crescent and waxing phases of the lunar cycle, and is representative of the period in a woman's life before she is able to bear children and produce life, as well as simply youth in general. This aspect most strongly represents the concept of growth and development, and is reflected in the waxing of the moon as it approaches its "full" stage, where it reaches its "peak" of potential, which can be connected to the middle stage of life when people are at their own highest points of potential, or the stage when a woman is able to give birth to new life, continuing the cycle of life. In the cycles of nature, the maiden is very commonly associated with the dawn, or sunrise, and the season of spring, when life begins to flourish and grow. The maiden can also be used, in this context, to represent the beauty of the creation of new life. She can also be associated with youth, and this connected to the ideas of innocence, growth, self-confidence, intelligence, learning, and gaining independence, as well as activities that are related to these concepts, such as creativity, discovery, exploration, and expression, as these are all things that normally happen during the early stages of one's life. Wiccans commonly worship the maiden form of the goddess as other goddesses that symbolize similar concepts, such as the Greek goddesses Artemis and Persephone, as well as Freya, a Norse goddess, and Rhiannon, a Celtic Goddess.

The next aspect of this cycle is the mother. The mother is associated with the full moon when the moon reaches its highest point, or its peak, and the fullest point in its cycle. This is, again, similar to the middle stage of life when people generally reach the height of their potential and will begin to realize that potential. This is also the time when women will generally be able to give birth and create a new life, as well, which fits in with the name of this form, the mother. This aspect of the Wiccan goddess is also associated with midday, and with the season of summer, when the day and the life that is created in the spring, respectively, reach their peak before beginning to descend to give way to new life, in the form of a new day or a new year. Summer is the lushest and vibrant season, during which the energies of life can be felt the most, with the fields and forests at their highest points, and hosting animals in similar stages of their lives, growing to maturity and becoming the most active. In human people, the mother is commonly associated with responsibility, adulthood, the fullness of life, and nurturing new life. As the stage at the "peak" of potential, both for the full moon and the life that it represents, the mother is very commonly considered within many different circles of Wiccans to be the most powerful of the three aspects of the goddess, and who most strongly represents the concept of the Wiccan goddess as a whole. Many Wiccans will commonly worship the mother in the form of various goddesses that typically symbolize similar, related concepts to the mother, such as the Greek goddesses Demeter and Selene, as well as the Celtic goddesses Danu and Badb and the Roman goddess Ceres.

Finally, the last form that the goddess takes is the crone. The crone is representative of the waning period of the lunar cycle. The crone was also referred to as the hag at one point. However, this was changed to the crone later on in order to fit the concepts and ideas that the crone embodies more clearly. The final aspect of the triple goddess represents the later part of life, when people generally slow down and begin to fade away in order to make room for new life to flourish, and of course, the part of a woman's life after which she has been able to give birth and has already created new life within the world. She is also associated with the seasons of autumn and winter, when trees and animals will begin to hibernate until the spring, as well as sunset and the night, when the day begins to "die down" in order to allow for that day to come to an end, bringing the new day in its wake. The crone is the wisest, eldest aspect of the triple goddess, and she represents aging, endings, death, and in some contexts, even things like a rebirth, past lives, transformations, guidance, prophecy, and vision of the future. Although this stage of life has been feared for millennia, and is still approached with apprehension and fear by a lot of people, the crone can serve as a reminder that death is simply a part of the cycle of life, just as the moon's waning period of the dark half of the year are necessary in order to allow for the new moon or spring and summer to take hold and create new life. If the crone does not play her very important role, then the maiden will not be able to begin to accept hers. The crone is most often represented by and worshipped in the form of various goddesses that are associated with death or the underworld, such as the Greek goddess Hecate, the roman Goddess Trivia, The Russian entity Baba Yaga, or the Celtic entities of the Cailleach or Morrigan.

The God and the Goddess are typically represented on the altar by a lot of Wiccan magic practitioners in a number of different ways that will vary based on their tradition or personal preferences. Some of the most common representations are candles. The god will usually be represented by candles with red, orange, yellow, or gold colors, whereas the Goddess will be represented by green, white, silver, or black ones. A lot of people will also use symbols to represent the appropriate deity. Common objects for the God are projective symbols like arrows, horns, spears, swords, and wands, whereas the Goddess will be represented by more receptive symbols like cauldrons or chalices, as well as representations of abundance, such as flowers or other kinds of plants. These can also be good ways to strengthen your connection with a particular deity or element during your spellwork for people who feel that they do not have a strong enough connection to those deities or elements.

A term that will be helpful to understand throughout this book is the "Wheel of the Year." The wheel of the year is a sort of calendar that outlines eight different major holidays or "Sabbats" that are commonly recognized within Wiccan practices. These eight sabbats are different occasions on which Wiccan practitioners will honor the roles of God and the Goddess in their cycle of sustaining life. The wheel itself is a representation of the cyclical relationships that are shared by the God and the Goddess, as well as the things that they represent such as the earth, moon, sun, and seasons. The wheel of the year, in this context, is representative of the cycles that the sun and the God follow around the earth with the passage of the seasons, and of course, the years, with the God's life cycle of dying in the autumn and winter, and being reborn and growing stronger in the spring and summer, as has been described earlier in this book. Each of the eight sabbats represents a different milestone signifying a particular point in the cycle that the earth takes in orbit around the sun. The first four of these eight sabbats are the Winter and Summer solstices Yule and Litha, and the spring and autumn equinoxes, Ostara and Mabon. The other four sabbats are the four points that fall in the middle of the points of the cross formed by the first four sabbats and are referred to as Beltane, Imbolc, Lammas, and Samhain.

Additionally, in this chapter, there have been several mentions of other gods and goddesses that Wiccans might worship or pray to, and that the Wiccan god and goddess are considered to encompass. This might seem a little bit confusing, but this is because, in Wicca and other forms of paganism, the "god" and "goddess" are all-encompassing entities that are used to describe the divine masculine and feminine energies that exist within the world and within the universe. For a lot of people who practice Wicca, these energies are also the source of or are embodied by a number of different deities that have existed within various different belief systems. In this sense, the concepts of the god and the goddess within Wicca are simple ways to explain the forces that exist in the universe in a way that is easy for people to understand and relate to. The God and Goddess are not so many literal entities that exist, so much as manifestations of various aspects of our world. Because of this, many of the gods and goddesses that exist within religions are "compatible" with the Wiccan concepts of the all-encompassing god and goddess. Many of these religions predate the modern concept of Wicca by thousands of years, but they have been "reclaimed" within Wiccans' belief systems by individuals and even groups who might feel a connection to those deities and religions. Of course, like many of the various aspects of Wicca and its practices, a lot of the ways that people tend to identify the divine forces that make up our world are very diverse and subjective.

For a lot of the people who practice Wicca and keep the "traditional," duotheistic concept of the god and goddess, these ancient deities are incorporated as distinct "lesser aspects" of the all-encompassing concepts of the god and the goddess. They do not play a role of their own but instead work as smaller, lesser parts of the god or goddess. Some people, however, might choose to include other deities into their concept of the God and Goddess, with a more "polytheistic" view of the world. These people might also include these deities as parts of their practices in addition to God and Goddess. They might choose to adopt specific deities as "patron" deities, with whom a person might maintain a specific relationship, or they might be honored by a person during specific points throughout the year. A person might also appeal to a specific deity or deities, reaching out for assistance with magical work or with specific types of magic that those deities are traditionally associated with.

Of course, it might seem a little bit off to "borrow" a specific deity or group of deities from another religion in order to worship in the context of your Wiccan practices, but the adoption of deities in this way is actually a somewhat old practice. Throughout human history, people have tended to merge or adopt various deities from the people that they come into contact with, even blending aspects of their own original religion with aspects from the new one. This can even be seen in Christianity in Ireland and Latin America, where a number of different pagan gods have been adopted to become Christian saints. A lot of Wiccans and other pagans will even maintain the perspective that all deities from all religions, and even the religions themselves, come from the same source and represent the same or similar ideals through slightly different lenses depending on the backgrounds or cultures of the people who "started" them.

As Wicca has evolved since its initial introduction in the 20th century, it has come to sometimes incorporate some of the deities who were worshipped in ancient times, like those from the ancient Celtic, Egyptian, Greek, and Roman pantheons, as well as other deities from sources like the Hindu and Norse pantheons. Most of the deities that have been mentioned in this book have also been from these sources. This might seem a little bit odd, as well, that there are only "ancient" deities being listed here, but there is actually a very good reason for that. Wiccans can technically work with deities from any pantheon, however, some people simply choose to only adopt specific deities as representations of their beliefs. A lot of people will only work with the deities from their own cultural heritage as a way of connecting with their ancestors, which could be a significant factor for this adoption of "old gods." However, there has also been a lot of discussion about the "appropriation" of deities from current existing, and even marginalized cultures being seen as insensitive, and the possibility of people from those cultures viewing the adoption (or appropriation) of their gods as a form of trivialization of the beliefs that they hold. Because of this, a lot of Wiccans will choose only to adopt deities from religions that have been "retired" in an effort to avoid upsetting or insulting the people who still practice the religions that those gods and goddesses come from. Ultimately, these decisions are personal, and mostly up to the individual.

If you do find that you would like to consider adopting and working with one or more additional deities from other sources, it can be important to do research in order to make sure that you maintain accuracy and stay faithful to the original purpose that those gods served and the religion they came from as a whole in order to avoid butchering or otherwise altering the spirit of those deities and religions. You might start by looking into your own lineage and researching the cultures that your ancestors came from, or even another specific part of the world or a particular culture that you are interested in. The gods that you choose to adopt, if any, are up to you, but you should try to do some research on them in order to get a better, clearer sense of the deity that you want to create a relationship with. If you read historical information about the people and the culture that those deities came from, this can be incredibly helpful in understanding a particular deity or pantheon. You should try to have as much information as possible, and get to know your gods and goddesses as much as you can. The relationship between a Wiccan, and even any person in general, and their deity or deities is an incredibly personal one and will vary from person to person.

Another concept that people are often confused by when it comes to the practices of Wicca and Wiccan magic is the actual nature of those practices. For people who practice Wiccan magic, the magic that they perform is not necessarily a "belief" or a "faith," so much as it is simply a practice. Wiccans don't necessarily need to have faith in or believe in magic, at least not in the typical mystical Harry Potter sense. Wiccan magic is simply a collection of various techniques that are used to help a Wiccan practitioner to work with the natural laws of the universe. The results of successful Wiccan magic can be literally experienced physically with a person's senses. This kind of magic is not entirely unique to Wicca, either, and not every Wiccan practitioner will practice magic. However, those who do should be extremely careful to only use spells that are not intended to harm other living beings within the earth or the earth itself. This is actually one of the first things that Wiccans typically learn when it comes to the practice of magic, as well, is the phrase "harm none." This phrase is often referred to as the only real "rule" within Wiccan practices. The "harm none" rule is the main concept behind what is typically referred to as the "Wiccan rede" and should be taken extremely seriously, as an act to enforce the core Wiccan ideal of living in harmony and maintaining a balance and equilibrium with all living things and with the earth itself.

A closely related concept to the Wiccan Rede is the Threefold law. This threefold law is also commonly referred to as the "rule of three." This "rule of three" is a significant part of many Wiccan traditions, but not all, and is entirely dependent on individuals and their circles. The threefold law is a general rule which states that every act that is sent out magically into the universe, whether positive or negative, will come back around to the person who sent them out three times over, or "three-fold." This is a very similar concept to the idea of "Karma," but with a slight twist of the addition of the multiplication of the return of the energy that is sent out by the user by three times.

Going back to the Wiccan rede, however, it is important to discuss in a little bit more detail. The Wiccan Rede is a very important rule and is usually one of the first concepts that a new Wiccan should learn, especially with regards to the practice of magic. The Wiccan Rede, as was mentioned before, is a very simple rule, and is commonly referred to as the only real "rule" that exists within Wicca. This rule is that Wiccans (in addition to all people in general, of course) should "harm none." As a practice that is centered around the earth and all of the life that exists on earth, one can easily see why a practice like Wicca would employ this simple concept as its "only rule." Being able to recognize and respect the power and the level of impact that you have as a magic user and as a person in general requires you to examine and evaluate your motives for your spells and magic, and making sure that you are avoiding any temptation that you might have to send out any energies that are meant to affect other people or beings negatively, as well as making sure that you do not have any ill intent with your magic or anything else that you do. This is why a lot of people who practice Wiccan magic will end their spells with phrases like "with harm to none" or "for the good of all" because you should never try to do harm to another living thing under any circumstances.

The full wording of the Wiccan Rede is commonly attributed to Doreen Valiente and its "An it harms none, do what ye will." Doreen Valiente is responsible for writing a large portion of the rituals for Gerald Gardner's original coven, and actually quoted this famous line in a speech that was recorded in 1964. The use of the word "an" can be confusing to a lot of people who are new to Wicca or who are unfamiliar with the word, but it is a simple word that most people can likely be able to pick up from the context, meaning something like how we would use the word "if" today. Of course, ye is a similar case, simply translating to the modern usage of the word "you." In common speech that someone might use in a regular conversation today, the sentence might read similarly to "As long as it doesn't hurt anyone, you can do what you want."

The Wiccan Rede is thought to have come from the mouth of Aleister Crowley, who once made a statement which was applied to his own religion, referred to as Thelema, and was quoted as "Do what thou wilt shall be the whole of the Law." It is also possible that the Wiccan rede came from the French play that was called the Adventures of King Pausole, in which the titular character King Pausole was heard instructing his subjects to avoid bringing harm to their neighbors, but that other than that, they can do what they like. While Gardner is apparently reported to have made explicit comparisons between the source of inspiration for the Wiccan system of morality and King Pausole, most Wiccan scholars typically believe that the Wiccan Rede was much more likely to have come from Aleister Crowley, as Crowley was a close friend of Gardner, and made a very significant impression on him over the course of that friendship. It is definitely possible that both of these sources had some level of impact over Gardner and over Wicca as a result, but regardless of its origin, the Wiccan Rede has become a very important aspect to the Wiccan system of morality and moral philosophy within the Wiccan practice.

The other important thing that Wicca teaches to the people who practice it is the "rule of three" or the "threefold law." This rule of three is not a part of all Wiccan traditions, but many Wiccans do recognize the rule of three. The rule of three essentially states that every action that you perform, especially for acts that are magical in nature, will be returned to you three times over, whether that act is positive or negative. The "three times" addition is an interesting part of this rule. For most Wicca practitioners, it simply means that the energies that you send out into the world will be applied to you as well, multiplied in intensity or frequency by three times. This serves as a little bit of motivation to perform positive acts, as well as a deterrent, meant to prevent people from bringing harm to others or performing any kind of action with ill intent. Gerald Gardner did not include the threefold law in his teachings of Wicca, although he was familiar with the rule of three. The rule of three was introduced at a later point by other witches who practiced Wicca after Gerald Gardner's teachings. Additionally, many people differ in their interpretation of the law of three, with some believing it to be a literal law of the world, while some people only seeing it as an encouragement to avoid bringing harm onto other people and beings and to encourage positive acts as well. Some people even choose to ignore it completely, sometimes following other similar concepts like the Law of Return or The Law of Cause And Effect as being far more accurate and effective ways to explain the concept of karmic exchange and its connections to the practice of magic. Regardless of a person's individual stance on it, the law of three can serve as a reminder that their actions will always have consequences, whether those will come in threes or not.

In addition to the concepts of the god and the goddess, many Wiccans will also follow the structure of the "classical" elements as general forces of nature. These elements are, of course, the air, earth, fire, and water, as well as the fifth element, spirit. These elements are generally accepted as the materials that make up the primary foundation upon which the universe is built. These elements are physically present in everything that exists throughout the world in some form or another. The four primary elements bind together all of the objects and the matter that exists within the world, while the fifth element of "spirit" or alternatively referred to as "akasha," is present in each of the other four elements. These elements are what make up the world and all of the things that exist within the universe, and are the acting forces of the cycle of eternal creation and destruction that is the basis for Wiccan beliefs and practices. These elements are also generally understood to make up the separate types of energies that are used in Wiccan practices of magic and are typically invoked at the beginning of a spell or other ritual in order to provide assistance with the magic that is being practiced.

Chapter 2: The Classical Elements And Spirit

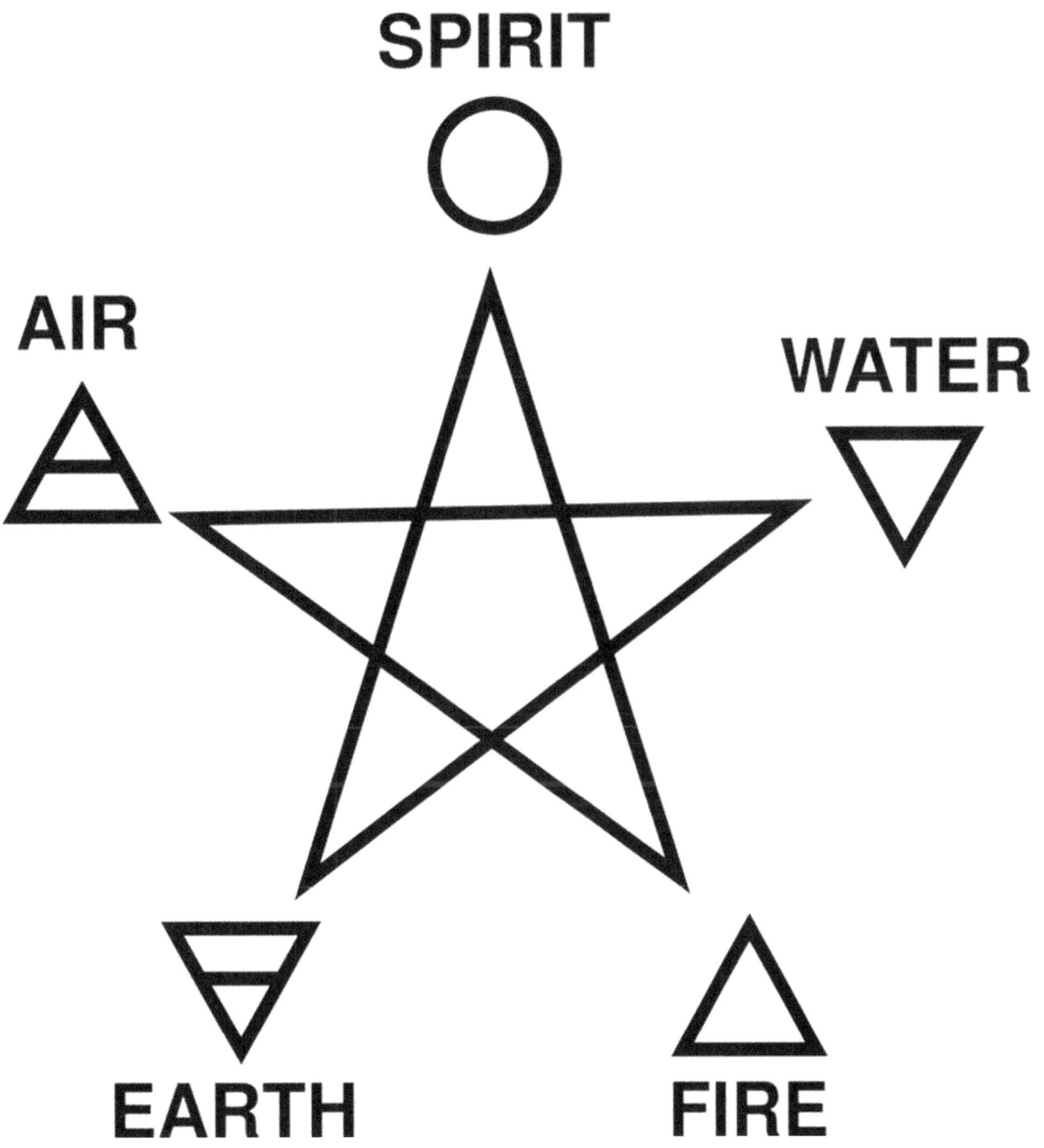

In order to understand the kind of magic that will be described in this book, it can be helpful to understand the fundamental rules that Wiccan magic follows and the basic concepts that make up those rules. In common Wiccan practices as well as many other pagan spiritual traditions, the elements are considered to be the basic fundamental foundations that all of the forces and matter within the universe are built on. These primary classical elements are the elements of Air, Earth, Fire, and Water, plus the fifth element, which is the Spirit. These five elements are present in everything that exists within the universe and are extremely important to the cycle of eternal creation and destruction that the Wiccan God and goddess follow. These elements are also the materials that make up all of the literal forces that govern everything that physically exists within the world, and as such are considered extremely sacred to the people who practice Wiccan magic. The elements are typically used in the practice of Wiccan magic and magical rituals and can even be considered by other people who live and work with the natural elements and the ways that they function. Every aspect of the material world and everything that exists physically within the world is bound together by and made up of the five elements of air, earth, fire, and water to varying degrees, with the fifth element of spirit being contained within each of the other four.

The concepts of these simple elemental states of physical matter have been a thing that people have considered since at least the time of the ancient Greeks. The four elements of air, earth, fire, and water were even commonly discussed by philosophers of that time and, of course, they were also adopted later on by alchemists for the practices that they employed in the practice of alchemy. The alchemists, and even greek philosophers, recognized that the four primary elements can be used as categories that all of the physical matter that exists within the world fall into and that nothing can physically exist that does not contain at least one of these four elements, or that can not be classified or categorized as or by using these four elements. Ancient Greeks even used these four basic elements as the basis for the development of their practice of medicine and healing within their society, as well as their spiritual beliefs and traditions. The four classical elements also influenced the discovery of all of the specific elements of modern chemistry that make up the world as we know them today.

The fifth element, "the spirit" is commonly referred to as "akasha" as well. This came from the origin of the concept of spirit as an element. A lot of different eastern astrological traditions also have a system of primary elements, but they are typically structured a little bit differently. For example, the Chinese astrological system contains two different elements that our western system of classical elements might consider as parts of the earth element as their own categories; wood and metal. The ancient Indian philosophers also had a similar structure in their own system of the classical elements, but with the fifth edition of the element called "akasha," which means "space." This term was borrowed a little bit later on by a number of western occultists and has been included in traditions and practices like Wicca to be used to refer to the "spirit" element. Another term that some people use instead of spirit or akasha is "aether," which was added to the original Greek system by Aristotle and essentially means something very similar to the element of spirit.

The five basic elements of air, earth, fire, water, and spirit are generally recognized by people who practice Wicca to be distinct representations of the different spiritual energies and are an incredibly important part of Wiccan magic rituals. The elements are usually invoked during the beginning phase of a Wiccan magic ritual in order to have them "participate" in the ritual and assist with the magical acts that are being performed. Additionally, all of the four primary basic elements each have their own cardinal directions that they are associated with, and a person who is practicing a magic ritual will usually physically turn to the corresponding direction in order to address the spirit of the element that they wish to invite into the circle and into the ritual. This is typically referred to as "calling the quarters" by Wiccan practitioners, or alternatively as simple "invoking the elements." Of course, the elemental energies that have been invoked will also need to be dismissed at the end of the ritual as well.

There are also other ways that the elements are represented in Wiccan magic rituals, as well. For example, there are a number of different tools that are typically used in these rituals that represent specific elements. These tools include things like the pentacle, which is representative of the element of the earth, a chalice (whether it is empty or full) can be used to represent the element of water, a wand can be used to represent the element of air, and a candle can be used to represent the element of fire. There are specific ways that you will need to handle these tools, however, so it can be important to remember to take care when handling tools like these. There are also other different kinds of tools that people will use in order to represent the different elements, depending on how elaborate the practice is of each individual person or even a circle of Wiccan practitioners, but it is usually recommended that at least one tool or other object used to represent each of the elements be present in the ritual. There are also other kinds of objects and tools that can be used to represent the different elements and their energies or spirits, like various different kinds of crystals, herbs, various objects, and even specific colors. You might want to use other kinds of objects, like a seashell to represent the element of water, a feather to represent air, a stone to represent earth, or ash or otherwise burned herbs to represent the element of fire. These objects will function slightly differently to the specific tools but will overall have the same general result of connecting the ritual that you are performing to the elements. It is recommended to take care and keep the meanings of the tools that you use to represent the different elements in mind in order to be able to achieve the desired results and properly invoke the elements during those rituals.

A lot of the people who practice Wicca will tend to adopt other additional occult traditions and practices into their own work. This can include things like astrology and tarot, as well as other practices and traditions that make use of the classical elements of air, earth, fire, and water to organize and classify their framework for knowledge. Things like the zodiac signs are very good examples of this, as each of the different signs is associated with its own element, allowing for the creation of four groups of three astrological signs that all relate to each other in terms of the elements that they represent. Once these associations and relationships between the different elements are understood, they can add a lot more depth to the interpretations that are made about how people who fall under the different astrological signs and by extension each of the classical elements will typically interact with each other. A good example of this is that the signs of fire and water as well as a fire sign and an air sign, just as the elements of fire and water might not mix very well, while fire and air do well together. In a similar way, the tarot deck has four suits that each represent one of the four classical elements, much like the astrological signs do. For example, the pentacle suit of the common tarot deck is typically associated with the element of earth, and the cards of that suit also relate to the concepts of prosperity and abundance, similarly to the earth itself.

Being able to work well with each of the four classical elements successfully will require you to be willing to learn more about those elements, as well as a willingness to develop your own personal relationship with the essence of each of the four elements in order to effectively "communicate" with the essences and "spirits" of each of those elements. You should try to read more about the classical elements and try to interact with them through your magic and in nature as much as you can in order to form a more direct connection with those elements and develop your bond to them.

The rest of this book will be focused primarily on candle magic and the things that are involved in that kind of magic. It is still incredibly important to go over all of the different elements, as they will be important when you are practicing candle magic as well. The first element that will be discussed here is air. The element of air is a very important one. Air is absolutely vital to our own day-to-day existence and being able to sustain life within our bodies, as without it, we would not literally be able to breathe and would fall within minutes. The oxygen in our air is what allows us to stay alive, fuel our fires, and go to places like Fiji when we are deathly afraid of aquatic forms of travel. The air is always present and is always around us, even if we (normally) can not see it. The air is only typically observable through the interactions that it has with the other three basic elements of earth, fire, and water, and the effects that it can have on those elements. The element of air is typically represented by things like the sky, clouds, wind, and the birds that travel through it. The air is also representative of a number of traits that exist within us, such as consciousness or the mind, intelligence, our ability to communicate with each other and other living beings, and the art of divination.

Air is fluid and is constantly moving and shifting, very similar to the element of water. It flows freely through the sky and rises and falls based on its own rules. The energies of the element of air can be especially capricious and can change quickly, just as the weather and the direction of the wind can fluctuate spontaneously and seemingly without warning. Of course, those who have a strong relationship with the element of the air and can understand it a little bit more easily can begin to gain a sense of the ways that it flows and the ways it communicates its movements. However, this element represents freedom and change, and those who are aligned with it should be careful to keep this in mind in order to keep up with the ways that it shifts and moves. Air is essential to life on earth, not only because it holds the oxygen that we breathe, but also because of the change that it brings. The air carries seeds and scatters them across the ground to help new plant life to take root within the earth, and it pushes the tides and stokes the fire that gives us a source of light and warmth. However, air can also be pushed to act in destructive ways. The air is the source of destructive forces such as tornadoes or other kinds of storms and can push temperatures to extremes, making cold colder and heat hotter. The air is an extremely capricious element and can push water to create hurricanes or encourage the fire to grow out of control. In small amounts, it is possible for the air to move the earth, but it can also be blocked by it. The earth is sometimes considered to be opposed by the element of air, and the two do not often mix very effectively.

The air can be incredibly varied in its strength and the ways that it is directed. Understanding such an enigmatic, difficult element can be difficult for those who do not have a strong connection to it. Of course, the air can supply us with life, and that is one of the simplest ways that you can use to connect with the element of air. Being conscious of your breath can be incredibly helpful in being able to relate to the air. There are a number of different kinds of breathing exercises and techniques that can help you to meditate on your connection with the air and enhance that connection. Taking a walk in a brisk wind can be helpful to others if they allow themselves to feel the wind and notice how the air moves along their skin. If you wish to improve your connection to the air, you should try to spend as much time as you can outside in contact with the air. Being able to appreciate the wind cooling your skin and moving through your hair on an especially hot day or watching the ways that the clouds and trees are moved by the wind can help you gain a stronger connection and a greater appreciation for the element of air.

The air is associated with the Wiccan deity of the god. As such, it carries masculine, projective energy as well. The direction that the air aligns with is the east, and some of the tools that are commonly used to represent the air are wands, incense, and bells. Its associated season is the spring, though the astrological signs that have the strongest connection to the air are Aquarius, Gemini, and Libra. The colors used to represent this element are Yellows, as well as silvers and whites. Air is most commonly involved in Wiccan rituals like smudging rituals or the burning of incense.

The next element is one that can be considered to be somewhat opposed to the element of the air, the earth. The element of earth is the foundation upon which all life on earth is supported by. In this sense, the earth can also be considered very similar to the air. Additionally, and also similar to the air, the earth element is ever-present throughout our world and is an incredibly versatile element, able to manifest as both the soil at our feet and the seeds that grow from it. Because of this, the earth is an incredibly important aspect of the eternal cycle of life that affects so many different aspects of Wiccan traditions and practices. Being represented by all of the different structures and the soil within the earth, as well as the forests and plant life that grows within them, the element of the earth is commonly associated with concepts such as abundance and prosperity, as well as rigidity and strength.

While the air is the element that supports all life in our universe, the earth is the source of all of that life, whether it takes the form of plants or animals. The earth also gave humans the clay and the stones that we originally used to make our tools, and the trees that we used to build our shelters and homes. Earth is a very strong and supportive element, which acts as a foundation for the other elements and improving their potential. However, the earth element can also be used as a destructive force and can take the form of terrible forces such as earthquakes or rock-slides in order to create "space" for new life to grow by pushing out the old.

The element of earth is capable of combining with the element of water, absorbing it or even being carved and changed by it. This is one of the few exceptions to the earth's unflinching and rigid nature, along with its relationship with the element of fire. The element of earth can be heated in order to allow it to become malleable and change form in order to create something new, or it can contain powerful forces like volcanoes, which can enhance the destructive nature of the earth to make way for fresh beginnings. As was mentioned before, however, the earth is sometimes opposed by the element of air, and the two do not typically mix in very effective ways because of their opposing nature. The earth is the most rigid and "grounded" of the four classical elements, providing a source of strength and stability to all of the life that rests upon and within it.

Because of the strength and stability that the earth can provide, and inspire us to strive toward, the earth can be an important element to connect with and gain a stronger relationship with. Some good ways to connect with this element are to immerse yourself in it and surround yourself with the earth element and its various forms. Hiking can be extremely effective for anyone, regardless of their particular environment, as the earth will be present in equal amounts in the forests and the deserts, as well as in the mountains or in caves. You can even find the earth in more developed, metropolitan areas in the form of parks, or even the buildings and tools that can be found in your surroundings.

Another good method that a lot of people, Wiccan or not, like to use to gain a stronger connection to the earth is to plant a garden. This is one of the easiest and most accessible ways that you can experience the grounding and healing energies of the earth. You can also do things like simply going out and being with the earth or laying down on the grass, meditating on the concepts that are associated with the earth and its energies. You should be making an effort to notice how your own energy will shift to a place of ease and peace when you are physically closer to and connecting with the energies of the element of earth.

The earth is associated with the Wiccan deity of the goddess, as opposed to the air's association with the god. As such, it carries feminine, receptive energy as well. The direction that the earth aligns with is the north, and some of the tools that are commonly used to represent the earth are the pentacle, as well as objects that literally contain the essence of the earth, such as bowls of salt or soil. Its associated season is the winter, though the astrological signs that have the strongest connection to the earth are Capricorn, Taurus, and Virgo. The colors that are used to represent this element are Yellows, similar to the air, as well as blacks, browns, and greens. Earth is most commonly involved in Wiccan rituals primarily by using salt to cast a circle before a ritual is performed. Sometimes, aspects of the element of the earth are also added to specific magical charms or as cleansing materials for crystals or other kinds of tools, as well as many spells, especially earth-centric ones, will have the practitioner bury specific objects in the earth.

The next element that will be discussed here will be the water. The element of water is commonly considered to be one of the most important elements for the existence of life. Of course, all of the classical elements are vital aspects of the creation and continuation of all life that exists in our universe, but later was one of the original sources of the development of life within the earth. All living things need it in order to continue to stay alive. It also guided us in similar ways to the element of fire and shaped the ways that we developed and grew over time. Before we build roads, we traveled along rivers and streams and built our towns around different bodies of water. The ocean makes up a very large portion of the planet Earth, and a large portion of the life on the planet is also hosted by the element of water. The water is very commonly associated with the moon, which controls its flow and tides, as well as things like dreams, emotions, and psychic abilities. The element of water is also extremely fluid and is constantly shifting, similar to the element of air and moves through the world quickly and efficiently by following the path of least resistance.

Unlike the air, the element of water can shift in form as well, being able to adopt the form of a solid as ice, or gas as small particles of water within the air. While the air moves around and shifts in location, water is considered to be the most adaptable of the four elements, able to take on different shapes as its environment requires. In cold climates, where things will typically remain still and the water is able to do the same, it will take on the form of ice. In an environment that does not support the water, it will move to a new location that can, which can be observed when the water rises as a gas, fall as rain or snow from the sky, and then evaporate as the earth heats up during the day. Water is represented by a number of different forms, each with its own degree of motion and fluidity. Forms such as ice, lakes, and oceans all move to some extent, but will mostly stay still and constant and able to support life, whereas the rain, rivers, and streams move more quickly and wash away impurities and heal. In these various forms and at various times, the element of water can be useful and be a representative of the cleansing, healing, nourishing, and purifying qualities that it can have.

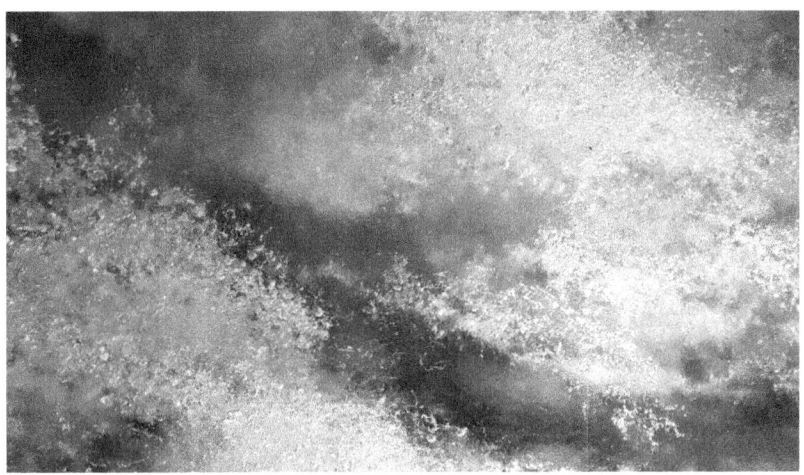

Water can also be dangerous in some forms, however. Just like the element of air, water can also be described as capricious at times. The element of water can work on its own or combined with other elements to create storms and hurricanes that can be incredibly dangerous to any creature unfortunate enough to be caught by them, as well as forces such as strong currents or riptides that can swallow living beings who aren't suited to handle them. Water is sometimes viewed as an opposing force to the element of fire, being able to extinguish open flames, and not usually being able to mix well with that element. The water element can also wash out and corrode the earth, and halt or encourage the air, depending on its form. Water is very likely the most versatile and flexible of the classical elements and can be used to both destroy and create in various ways depending on its application.

Because of its incredibly fluid and shifting nature, the element of water can be somewhat difficult to understand for some people. One very obvious way that you can strengthen your connection to the element of water is to go for a swim. Natural bodies of water are ideal, of course. A lake, river, pond, or even the ocean can be extremely helpful to people who want to gain a sense of the different rhythms of this element and the ways that it moves, but you can also use a swimming pool if you prefer or only have access to that. When you are swimming, you should be trying to actively notice how you feel before, during, and after the time that you spend literally exposed and immersed in this element, in order to gain a better sense of the energies of the element of water. You might also try to use the different forms of water to form a connection. You could go out in the rain and feel it on your skin, or do the same during a shower. You can try to actively appreciate the water that you drink and appreciate the healing properties that it has, and notice how much better you will feel if you are staying properly hydrated. Water is one of the more versatile elements and can be connected to in more varied ways than the other elements, so you should try different things and different methods of strengthening your connection to it in order to find out what works best for you.

The element of water is associated with the Wiccan deity of the goddess, similar to the earth, because of its ability to create and sustain life as well as its connection with the moon. As such, it carries feminine, receptive energy as well. The direction that water aligns with is the west, and some of the tools that are commonly used to represent this element are the cauldron or the chalice. Its associated season is autumn, though the astrological signs that have the strongest connection to the earth are Cancer, Pisces, and Scorpio. The colors that are used to represent this element are black, like with the earth, as well as blue and indigos, and greens. Water is most commonly involved in Wiccan rituals primarily by using a black bowl filled with water or other liquids for scrying, or divination. Water is also used in most teas, as well as in potions and various different kinds of spells.

The fourth element that will be discussed here will be fire. The element of fire is considered to be one of the most mesmerizing of the four classical elements, but it can also be the most volatile. If you've ever gotten too close to a fire or bumped into a hot stovetop, you might have realized that fire can be very dangerous to even come in contact with in any way. However, while this is definitely true, the element of fire has been incredibly helpful to humans and our development throughout the years. We did survive without the use of fire, but since its discovery, our existence has become much more comfortable and healthy. This element has allowed us to become much more capable and able to survive and even thrive in almost any kind of environment. The use of fire has allowed us to continue to work and stay active after the sun falls, stay comfortable and living in colder climates, and even develop new skills such as cooking and metalworking.

The element of fire is very commonly represented by the sun and the light and warmth that it produces, because of the same aspects that can be found in fire, and the assistance and comfort that both things have given to humankind. However, it is also related to things like the stars, deserts, and volcanoes for their destructive and volatile nature. Fire is typically seen as the element that most directly represents transformation. This idea was touched upon in the section about water and its ability to adapt, but water typically primarily changes itself. Fire enables, and even sometimes forces change within other objects. This can be seen when you cook food such as meat, the way it can evaporate water, or meltdown ores and minerals to create stronger forms of the earth-like metals. The element of fire is also commonly associated with similar concepts like illumination, vitality, and creativity. Unlike the earth, and even water, the element of fire is constantly in motion. Fire is literally made up of particles that shift and vibrate rapidly, causing friction, and even when it is tethered to a specific spot, it continues to be the most active and energized of the four classical elements. Fire represents energy and activity in this sense and is a powerful force that breathes life and acts as a catalyst for change and transformation in everything it comes in contact with. Of course, this change can also sometimes be harmful or destructive as well. This is the reason for fire being seen as such a terrifying force, causing some animals to become fearful or apprehensive toward it, and why it literally causes pain to animals or people who come in contact with it directly. Fire can be put out or extinguished by all of the other elements, depending on their application, but it can also be fueled by those elements, feeding on wood or other substances from the earth and being made stronger by air or flammable oils and other liquids.

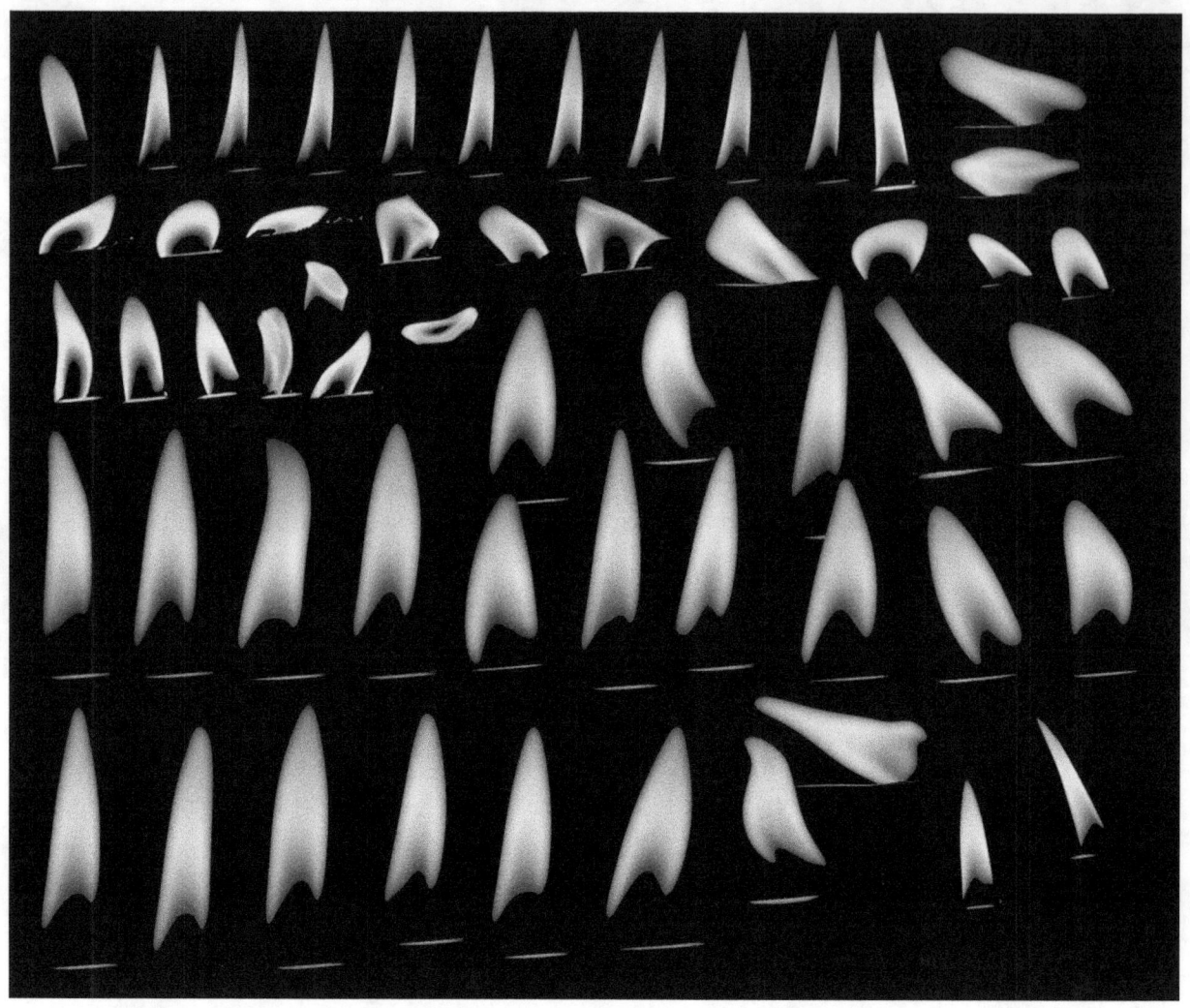

Fire is very unlike the other four classical elements in that it is pure and very easy to understand. The energies of the element of fire are simple because fire only exists as its energies, of which there is only a handful at best. However, it can still be very difficult to understand because of the hazards and dangers inherent in its handling and use. Because of the dangerous and volatile nature of the element of fire, it can be difficult to get close enough to be able to strengthen your bond to the element. One method that you could use is to try to be near a source of fire, as long as you are also making sure to be safe about it. Maybe sit outside by a campfire or bonfire, trying to pay attention to it and feel its warmth and the ways that it shifts and moves. You should also try to listen to the ways that the flame crackles off of the wood that fuels it or watches the embers as they float through the air before they fizzle out, meditating to the energies that the fire produces and the way that it changes the elements that surround it. If you do not have a safe place to create a flame outside, you might try doing the same on a smaller scale with the flame of a candle or in a fireplace. These sources will obviously be smaller and more contained, making it a little bit more difficult to understand the ways that the element of fire affects the other elements and is affected by those elements, but you can still learn from it and be able to strengthen your bond to the element even with a smaller flame. Another very helpful source of flame and the energies produced by the fire element is, of course, the sun. You might try to go outside and spend time feeling and experiencing the warmth and the light that the sun produces in order to gain a better understanding of its energies.

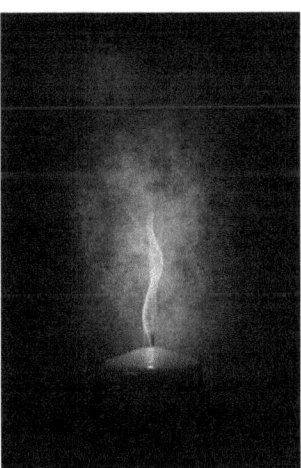

The air is associated with the Wiccan deity of the god. As such, it carries masculine, projective energy as well. The cardinal direction that fire aligns with is the south, and some of the tools that are commonly used to represent the air are athames (ceremonial knives, usually with black handles) or wands, as well as things like candles. Its associated season is the summer, though the astrological signs that have the strongest connection to the air are Aries, Leo, and Saggitarius. The colors used to represent this element of fire are whites, similarly to the element of air, and opposite to earth and water, as well as golds, oranges, and reds. The element of fire is used in the form of various types of candles to enhance the atmosphere of the environment used for spells and magic rituals, and additionally as the primary focus for candle spells.

There is also a fifth element, as has been mentioned briefly in this book. Of course, the four classical elements of air, earth, fire, and water which all make up all of the physical matter and essential force that governs our world, but each of those elements in their various forms also contain the element of "spirit," which is sometimes referred to as "akasha." The fifth element of spirit is present and exists within all of the things that exist within the world, but it cannot be experienced or felt in a literal sense. The element of spirit does not exist on its own, it only exists within the other elements and acts as the force that balances and binds the other elements to each other. The spirit element can be thought of as being similar to the bonds or forces that govern the ways that the elements act within our world. The element of spirit is what you will usually be used in magic rituals to invoke the god and goddess, as well as the four classical elements as they are needed. The element of spirit exists within us as people, as well as all other living things within the world, whether we or they are aware of it or not. When you gain an awareness of the element of spirit, this might manifest as a clear and focused sense of drive within us, or what we might call "determination" or other similar concepts. When you have a strong connection to the spirit element, you can use it to manifest within you and in the world as "change," through your magical work and even in non-magical ways, to some degree.

The concept of a fifth element was introduced in ancient Greece by Aristotle, who thought that there was something missing from the four classical elements. The Greeks were very spiritual, and a lot of them didn't completely agree with the structure of the four elements. They worshipped a number of different deities and recognized the presence of the divine, so it seemed apparent to them that there was more than just physical matter to be taken into consideration. They introduced the concept of the "aether" to what they thought of as "upper air," or the gods' air. This is what would sustain the lives of their deities, and was originally thought of as another part of the element of air, but they realized that that didn't completely fit, and made "aether" its own element which would make up the fifth point on the pentagram's star. A lot of Wiccans today even use the word "aether" to refer to the fifth element. Another common name for it is "akasha," which is a Sanskrit word that translated to English as "space." Of course, this element of akasha is not meant to represent the vacuum outside of our world, but the intangible energy that exists in all forms of matter within our universe. Akasha is also viewed as the "first" element and the source of all of the matter within our universe. Because of its nature, the element of spirit can sometimes be difficult for us to understand. It is hard for us to observe it, since it isn't represented by a physical object that we can hold, like earth or water, or a force that we can feel, like air or fire. The spirit can be especially difficult to keep in mind during our busy lives in our noise and distracting modern world, but it can become much more apparent when things are quiet and still, and especially when we are focusing on magical energies within ourselves and the elements. During spellwork and meditation, a lot of people will find that they will be able to notice this element much more easily, and will be able to form a much stronger bond with this element.

The element of spirit is also very unlike the other primary classical elements in that since it cannot exist on its own, only within the other elements, it does not have its own specific associations for the purposes of magic or magical rituals. There is one exception to this, in that the element of spirit can sometimes be represented by the color white, similarly to the potential that white light has in containing all of the other colors in our visible spectrum. However, the spirit element does not have any connections or associations, aside from the color white, to any different directions, energy types, genders, or objects like each of the other four elements. The element of spirit is representative of divine intelligence, which is why it does not have any specific connections to symbols or tools like the other elements. However, the pentacle is a common point of discussion in connection to the Wiccan elements. On the pentacle, which is made up of five points surrounded by a circle, the element of spirit is typically represented by the top point, or as the circle that binds all of the other four elements and the world to each other.

62

Chapter 3: Wiccan Candle Magic

The concepts and practices of magic do not belong to any specific religious or spiritual tradition. There are many different cultures that have developed their own magical practices, like the hoodoo tradition that belonged to African people who were brought to the Americas and that was developed based on their original African religious practices, as well as the Egyptian magical practice of Heka or the healing work of curanderos from Latin America. Magic can be practiced by any person of any religious background or set of beliefs. Wiccan practices and traditions, specifically, most magical practices are based on the practices of the folk healers from Europe, as well as the ancient Hermetic philosophies that were rediscovered during the Renaissance. But while there are a number of different spells and methods that have been passed down over the generations, the magic practices in Wicca is not typically considered to be a static art. There are new and different spells and approaches to those spells to help manifest the magical energies that are being developed and realized constantly. People who are willing to experiment with their magical practices are always finding new ways of doing so, and of using the various natural energies that make up the world and the various elements that exist within it.

There are a lot of different kinds of magic and magical traditions that Wiccans from different places or "schools" use, from things like divination in the form of scrying or even tarot readings and energy clearings or ritual dances, and even in different forms of more hands-on magic practices like creating magical charms and other kinds of tools for harnessing magical energies. Additionally, there are a lot of different kinds of ingredients or materials that are used in magical work and magic practices from a number of different sources, like things that you might imagine as being "magical" or connected to the typical "witch" figure, like cast-iron cauldrons or wands, to even mundane objects like stones and ribbons, or even simple tools like incense, bowls of earth or water, or candles to represent the elements. Every individual person and even specific circles of people who practice magic in these ways will have their own preferences and styles for these kinds of things, as magic is ultimately a very personal art that will vary from person to person. Regardless of the specifics of a person's particular brand of magic practice, there are a few forms of Wiccan magic that are fairly consistently popular among Wiccan practitioners, and could be good starting points for new people who are learning about magic as well as seasoned "magic users" who are wanting to explore new methods.

The first of these methods is candle magic. This is the specific kind of magic that will be covered throughout the majority of this book. Candle magic is a great starting point for new people who are wanting to explore the realm of magic and practicing spellwork Candle magic is one of the most simple and straightforward types of magic, as well as one of the most easily accessible. A basic candle spell can help newcomers to the realm of magic and magical practice to "work out their magical muscles" and strengthen their bonds to the god and goddess and the energies that weave themselves through the world around us. These work, essentially, by allowing you to "channel" your magical intention through the candle's flame. As the candle burns and disappears, it leaves the material plane and into the etherial one, carrying the request or message of your magical intention with it. This physical transformation of the candle can be extremely helpful to new Wiccans and magical practitioners because it is a physical tool that can be used to help you to visualize the process of manifestation.

Another very popular form of magic that people commonly practice is crystal magic. Crystal magic is another very popular way that a lot of people use to become familiar with some of the most beautiful and mysterious creations of nature. Crystals are technically inorganic but are still a very important part of the world and many witches and healers do consider them to be "alive," in a sense. Crystals can impart powerful healing energy to animals, people, and even plants because of their connection to the elements and to the forces that bind the elements together. Crystals can be extremely effective conduits for energy and can help us to manifest our magical intention in a similar way to a candle. A magic practitioner can use crystals in this way to channel and manifest their magical intent into the world through the energy field of the crystals they use in this way, making these very versatile tools very effective for all kinds of different spells.

Another useful kind of magic that is also very accessible, depending on your environment, of course, is herbal magic. Herbal magic is a very practical kind of practice. Most herbal magic can be performed with various kinds of ingredients and tools that you will probably already have access to in your kitchen at home, making this one of the most immediately accessible kinds of magic to be used on the fly. Herbs are also considered to be some of the most versatile magical "tools" for more hands-on magical applications, as well. You can use these resources to create your own magical crafts. Like dream pillows, poppets, sachets, spell jars, and a number of other different kinds of magical charms as well. Some people will even create their own incense and oils with different kinds of herbs, which can add even more magical power to the spellwork and different magical applications that they utilize. Herbal magic is often one of the first kinds of magic that a new practitioner will learn because of the accessibility and ease that comes with it, and its nature as one of the most rewarding forms of the craft, as well.

While these candles, crystals, and herbs are some of the most commonly used ingredients and tools that are used in Wiccan magic practices and traditions, there are other objects and tools that Wiccan practitioners will keep around, that can also be incredibly useful. These include things like incense, tarot cards, and oils. Incense is a very old tool that people use to represent the element of the air. Additionally, it can draw on the aromatic nature of various herbs, oils, spices, and other things to help a magic practitioner to create a much more effective atmosphere for their magical practices and help them to achieve a state of mind that is conducive to a stronger connection with the ethereal world. As well as commonly being burned during formal Wiccan rituals, many people will often burn incense during spellwork, because of the scented smoke and its ability to facilitate positive and effective state of mind for working with magic, as well as the many qualities that incense is thought to have like increasing focus and concentration, as well as your connection to the world around you.

Another tool that many people will use for and during their magical practices are oils. These are a very important component of magical practice and rituals for a lot of people, who will use these magical oils to anoint the tools that they use during these practices, like their amulets, crystals, ritual tools, talismans, and even themselves and their own physical bodies. Essential oils are commonly used in the creation of things like incense, and can also be helpful and useful for candle magic and the creation of charms, as well. Most, if not all magical acts and practices can be made more effective with the use of these kinds of oils, either on their own or combined with other kinds of oils, depending on the intent and personal preferences of the person who is using them.

Tarot cards are also another popular kind of tool that people will use, specifically for purposes like divination. Other kinds of tools that are commonly used for divinatory purposes are crystals, scrying mirrors, or runes. Tarot cards are some of the most popular tools used for divination, which can sometimes be considered to be its own form of magical application, but tarot cards are also used for other kinds of spellwork and magical practice as well. For example, you might display the moon card from a tarot deck on your altar whenever a full moon spell is being executed. A prosperity spell might include the use of the king or queen of the pentacles suit, or even the sun card. Some people even consult the tarot before they design a particular spell as well, in order to best understand the intention that they might have or want to have, and how to best use the spell.

The specific kind of magic that will be focused on in this book will be candle magic. Candle magic is often thought to be one of the oldest forms of magic to be practiced by human people, and whether or not this belief is actually true, it is undeniable that fire was considered to be sacred by our ancestors, who would honor their deities with things like candles, torches, and other tools to contain and carry flames. The discovery of the creation of fire was obviously a very big step that humankind took on the way to civilization and the development of different tools and other technologies, and was the only source of light that we had control over, allowing us to use it to be able to stay active when the sun and moon did not provide enough light for us to do so. The element of fire has been an extremely important part of our growth and development as a species, and it can be very easy to see why this power has been a symbol of sacred power throughout our time on the earth.

Of course, those are not the only uses that the element of fire has had for humankind. Our use of this element went beyond simply providing a source of light and warmth to help to keep us alive. Over time, we learned to harness it and use the power of fire to be able to heat metals in order to shape them and even make them stronger and more durable, and to make things like the candled that we still use today, as well as for entertainment and ritual uses, even making it a somewhat trivial aspect of our daily lives. After all, when was the last time you didn't live somewhere with an air conditioner or electricity? These inventions were only possible because of the element of fire and the ways that we developed to be able to harness it. However, the element of fire is still seen as somewhat special in our everyday lives. People love candles, even though we have access to other sources of heat and light, and even ones that can usually be much more effective. There are also a number of religious ceremonies and services that make use of candles in a number of different ways, as well. We even use them on specific occasions, like on birthdays, to pay homage to the transformative power of the element of fire. This might also be why so many people who are curious about or interested in beginning to practice magic are so drawn to candle magic. Candle flame can be very effective in creating a pleasant atmosphere, and fire has been such an important part of our lives, it just makes sense that we are drawn to it in this way. The fire has an almost hypnotic way of making a lot of people feel more at ease by simply looking into a flame and watching it dance and flicker, almost as if it is a living being. Lighting candles is also commonly seen as one of the easiest ways that we can begin to transition from our typical, ordinary reality and begin to connect with the energies of the world around us, whether in the context of magical tradition and practice or not.

Because of this connection that the element of fire can provide to us with the energies and spirits of the elements, candle magic is one of the best starting points for people who are beginning to practice magic in general, and why many Wiccans are so fond of candle magic in particular. A basic candle spell can help newcomers to the realm of magic and magical practice to "work out their magical muscles" and strengthen their bonds to the god and goddess and the energies that weave themselves through the world around them, and can allow people to be able to more easily and effectively focus on and direct their energy into their magical intention when they perform this kind of magic. Candle magic works, essentially, by allowing you to "channel" your magical intention through the candle's flame. As the candle burns and disappears, it leaves the material plane and into the etherial one, carrying the request or message of your magical intention with it. This physical transformation of the candle can be extremely helpful to new Wiccans and magical practitioners because it is a literal physical tool that can be used to help you to visualize the process of manifestation of the energies that you are putting out into the world.

A candle can be a very effective and balanced symbol or representation of the elements. Of course, this includes fire, but also the other three elements as well. The wick and the base of a candle are effective representations of the element of earth, as they are both made up of different aspects of the literal element of earth, as well as the ways that they are able to keep the flame grounded and support it as well. The wax can be an effective representation of the element of water, as it also transforms from a solid to a liquid, and then becomes a gas, in the same way, that water does when it is exposed to heat and can be a symbol of the shifting and changing nature of the element of water. The element of air is represented by the oxygen that keeps the flame alive, as well as the smoke that comes from the burning wick and the wax as the earth and water separate to temporarily become a part of the air. Of course, the flame itself is an aspect of the element of fire, being a literal flame. The spirit is even represented in candle magic when you charge the candle with your intention and action to send that magical energy off into the world.

Candles have a lot of symbolic qualities that can be used to represent the way the elements work, but they can also vary in color as well. The colors of different objects, and especially candles, can be used for different effects based on the color of the candle.

Certain colors are commonly associated with different forces or qualities, like luck, love, wealth, and even by death. There are certain colors that are very directly apparent, like the color red, which has always seemed to be associated with things like love and passion and even anger, in certain specific contexts. The color green is also commonly associated with things like abundance and growth, like the colors of the earth and the plants that grow within it. Being able to use these colors in your practice of candle magic can help to reinforce the intention that you might have for the spell that you are performing. There are even specific candles that are designed explicitly for use in things like candle magic, which are aptly referred to as "spell candles." These can be found in almost any color, and are very common and easy to find in relevant shops. Some of the different common colors that are typically used in the practice of candle magic, as well as their meanings, will be listed below:

• Red: Red is commonly viewed as the color that most accurately embodies concepts like courage, strength, passion, and emotion. These might take the form of anger, or as valor or determination. Whatever the context, red is a color that represents intensity. This color is most often used in the practice of candle magic to represent concepts such as love, health, physical energy or strength, or willpower.

- Orange: Orange is commonly viewed as the color that most accurately embodies concepts like attraction, energy, stimulation, and vitality. These can be similar to the color red, which makes sense since it is a similar color, even in a literal visual sense. The energies of this color might take the forms of eagerness, excitement, or alertness. Whatever the context, orange is a color that represents stimulation and vitality. This color is most often used in the practice of candle magic to represent concepts such as encouragement, power, or the ability to adapt to one's surroundings, especially those that are new or unfamiliar.

- Yellow: Yellow is commonly viewed as the color that most accurately embodies concepts like Intelligence, knowledge, inspiration, and even imagination. Yellow is a bright color, often being used to represent the sun or other sources of light or inspiration. The energies of this color might take the forms of positivity or confidence. Whatever the context, Yellow is a color that represents the ability to learn and to study, as well as the ability to communicate. This color is most often used in the practice of candle magic to represent concepts such as communication and confidence, as well as the ability to gain new knowledge in the forms of study and even through divination.

- Green: Green is commonly viewed as the color that most accurately embodies concepts like Growth, abundance, and balance, as well as things similar to wealth and renewal. Green is a very positive color, often being used to represent plant life and the concepts of growth and prosperity. Whatever the context, Green is a color that represents luck and prosperity, as well as the ability to grow and develop. This color is most often used in the practice of candle magic to represent concepts such as prosperity, employment, health, and good luck, as well as things like fertility, balance, and renewal.

- Blue: Blue is commonly viewed as the color that most accurately represents concepts like protection and peace, as well as things like wisdom and truth. Blue is a very calm and deep color, often being used to represent things like harmony, healing, psychic abilities, and understanding. Whatever the context, Blue is a color that represents peace and understanding. This color is most often used in the practice of candle magic to represent concepts such as peace, wisdom, psychic ability, healing, and stability.

- Violet: Violet is commonly viewed as the color that most accurately represents concepts like spirituality, devotion, and idealism. It is also sometimes used to represent concepts similar to those of blues like wisdom and peace. Violet is a very calm and deep color, similarly to blue as well. Whatever the context, violet is a color that represents spiritualism and devotion. This color is most often used in the practice of candle magic to represent concepts such as spiritualism, devotion, idealism, divination, and the enhancement of nurturing qualities.

- White: White is commonly viewed as the color that most accurately represents concepts like innocence and purity. It is also sometimes used to represent concepts like peace and purity, similarly to some of the qualities of blues and yellows. White is a very pure and innocent color. This color is most often used in the practice of candle magic to represent concepts such as clarity, cleansing, spiritual growth and understanding, purification, and even order or stability.

- Black: Black is commonly viewed as the color that most accurately represents concepts like dignity and force. As the opposite of the previous color of white, black is commonly used to represent similarly opposed concepts like stability and protection, in the form of the banishment of negative energies. This color is most often used in the practice of candle magic to represent concepts such as powerful forces, the banishment or removal of negative energies, enlightenment, or transformation.

- Silver: Silver is a color that is very similar to some of the aspects of other colors that have been listed here. The color of silver is most commonly used to represent concepts and qualities such as intelligence, memory, wisdom, and even psychic abilities. This color is most often used in the practice of candle magic to represent concepts such as the development of spiritual or psychic abilities, as well as meditation and warding off negative energies.

- Gold: Gold is a color that is very similar to some of the aspects of other colors that have been listed here. The color of gold is most commonly used to represent concepts and qualities such as inner strength, self-realization, and intuition. This color is most often used in the practice of candle magic to represent concepts such as ambition, finances, fortune, health, success, and even divination.

- Brown: Brown is a color that is very similar to some of the aspects of other colors that have been listed here. The color of brown is most commonly used to represent concepts and qualities such as endurance, grounding, and strength. This color is most often used in the practice of candle magic to represent concepts such as balance, concentration, animal companions, the home, and material gains and possessions.

- Grey: Grey is a color that is very similar to some of the aspects of other colors that have been listed here. The color of grey is most commonly used to represent concepts and qualities such as stability, neutrality, and reserve, as well as things like contemplation and introspection. This color is most often used in the practice of candle magic to represent concepts such as complicated or difficult decisions or compromise.

- Indigo: Indigo is a color that is very similar to some of the aspects of other colors that have been listed here. The color of indigo is most commonly used to represent concepts and qualities such as emotion, fluidity, expressiveness, and insight. This color is most often used in the practice of candle magic to represent concepts such as meditation, purpose, and spirituality.

- Pink: Pink is a color that is very similar to some of the aspects of other colors that have been listed here. The color of pink is most commonly used to represent concepts and qualities such as affection, companionship, and friendship. This color is most often used in the practice of candle magic to represent concepts such as friendships, romantic relationships, or other kinds of partnerships, spiritual healing, and awakening.

Chapter 4: Cleansing Your Candles

Once you have decided on what kinds of candles you will be using for your candle spells, you might want to cleanse them as well, before you actually use them for your rituals or spells. Cleansing is a topic that gets mentioned a lot with regards to Wiccan magic practices, but can also be somewhat vague, making it somewhat difficult to understand for people who might be unfamiliar with the concept, or who are new to Wiccan magic practices. Regardless, the act of cleansing is very important for new Wiccans and magic practitioners to learn about and how to perform.

There are a number of different methods that people use, and a number of different reasons that people might have for cleansing their tools, and many of these methods and the reasons behind them are described in vague, roundabout ways, making it even more difficult to understand. However, once you understand the basic concepts behind it, the topic of cleansing can be a very sensible one and will become much easier for you during your magic rituals and other practices. The only thing that will be preventing you from doing so is whether you are able to remember to do it. A lot of people can simply forget to cleanse as much as they probably should, or might simply neglect this step of the process. Maintenance can be one of the less interesting aspects of any art, but it is an extremely important one and is what typically separates the good from the great. It can be too easy to forget to cleanse your home or your tools every so often, just as with a car or... well, a tool, until it becomes too late.

A lot of people might even have some misconceptions about what cleansing is, or might misunderstand the basic purpose of the act of cleansing. A lot of people tend to view the act of cleansing as something similar to "banishing evil spirits" or "grounding," but these aren't necessarily the case at all. Cleansing is simply the act of removing negative or otherwise unwanted energies from a person, place, or object. In this context, of course, it will be used for objects like your candles and other tools, but it can apply to most other things as well. Cleansing is usually also the gentlest and most careful form of removing these unwanted energies, unlike banishment, which is a much more forceful strategy. Cleansing differs from things like banishment, as instead of forcefully removing the unwanted energies or entities to get rid of them, you are simply getting rid of the bonds that tie the energy to that place or thing and allowing that energy to become something more neutral or even positive. This is a very useful practice to help you to make sure that your environment or things within your environment are "clean" and do not have any kinds of energies that could potentially be harmful to you in any way. Cleansing is a good method for being able to clear out your environment and surrounding objects, essentially helping you to create a "blank slate." This is also useful for preparing your tools and ingredients for spell work or for keeping your own energy healthy and stable. A lot of people who practice Wiccan magic like to make sure to periodically be cleansing their home and objects around their home in order to maintain this positive energy, as well as making sure to cleanse new objects that they might bring into their home, too, in order to rid it of any unwanted energies as quickly as possible and avoid bringing those energies into the home.

Cleansing an object or space of energies is a very useful skill that you can use for a number of different reasons. Cleansing, of course, is very different from banishment, as it is a much gentler method for clearing out any unwanted energies. A lot of people will typically cleanse their home at a rate of once every few weeks, in addition, to immediately after any kind of stressful or otherwise emotionally significant or impactful event, as these kinds of events can disrupt the energies of your home and the objects within it. You might want to cleanse your home or various objects that you own more or less often, as well, depending on how receptive or sensitive you are to the energies of objects and places, or if you are particularly prone to things like mood swings or any sort of emotional distress is common for you. The frequency at which you should perform these cleanses will vary depending on you and your personal preferences.

Some people might even periodically take time out to cleanse their own energies as a way to help avoid any "buildup" of unwanted or unpleasant energies. You might find that this is very helpful to you, or you might not find it necessary to cleanse yourself as often. Luckily, it isn't actually that hard to do this, so you won't need to go too far out of your way to cleanse your own energy. You don't have to do any kind of complicated ritual or smoke cleansing in order to clear out any lingering energies. A lot of people will even perform a simple water cleansing in the shower, which can be a very good time and place. Many cultures have been known to prefer to bathe in specific ways as a way to incorporate simple cleansing rituals into their regular daily routines. You can even use a simple act like washing your hands in your sink as a short, simple way to cleanse your energy, or you might do things like immersing yourself in the elements by standing or lying in the grass or carrying effective cleansing stones like smokey quartz with you. A lot of the normal methods of cleansing energies can be applied to yourself very easily and without much trouble. Of course, you might not want to bury yourself in the sand for a day, but whatever method works for you will do fine.

The first thing you should do when cleansing your objects is to decide on what you will be cleansing. In this case, this will be your candles, but you might also want to try cleansing some of the other things that you own like tools or even your house in general, in order to help make it a more inviting or comfortable space. You might want to do so if the energy within your home feels a little bit stagnant or unusual for some reason. This can also apply to specific objects that you own. You might notice weird energy from a new thing that you picked up or received as a gift from a friend, or it might just not "feel like you" yet if it is new in your home. In these cases, the new or unfamiliar objects can tend to stick out, like a sore thumb. You might even wake up and realize that you feel a little bit drained or off-center one day. In these situations, you should try cleansing your home and the things that you own.

Next, you will want to determine the method that you will be using for this cleansing. There are a large number of different ways that different people will go about cleansing, but it is important to choose the right one for your goals and the things that you are trying to cleanse at a given time, as well. For example, you might not want to use water for something like a crystal, especially if that crystal is soluble in the water and will dissolve. This includes things like malachite which can actually become toxic in the water, opals, and pearls which can lose their luster and even break, and lodestones which will rust when exposed to water. There are also other factors, like pets. If you use smoke or other similar kinds of methods of cleansing in a room with a bird or other small pet, this can damage their respiratory systems, especially with birds, which can be incredibly sensitive to smoke. Each different method has a specific kind of time and place that will be the safest in which to perform it and will allow it to be as effective as possible, so it can be very important to choose the method of cleansing that you will be used carefully and wisely.

One method that a lot of people like to use for cleansing is what is commonly referred to as "recaning." Recaning is also referred to as "smoke cleansing," and is simply the process of cleansing by using smoke. This is most often used for large areas or spaces, but can also be used for specific objects or even yourself. Sage is the most common tool used for recaning, but there are a number of different materials that people will use fairly commonly for recaning as a cleansing method, like incense, cedar, palo santo, and a number of other different kinds of herbs.

The process of cleansing with smoke is a fairly simple and straightforward one. You will want to begin by lighting the herbs or other materials that you are using so that a nice group of embers forms in order to continue to produce the smoke that you will be using, making sure to blow out any active flames, which will burn the sticks or bundles too quickly, making them slightly less effective. You want to have a nice smolder at the end, but not a flame. Once your materials are smoldering, you will want to waft the smoke that is produced around the object or the room that you are cleansing, allowing the smoke to permeate and break up any unwanted or unpleasant energies, allowing them to return to their normal, neutral state as freely flowing energies.

It is also important to remember that this is not what people commonly (and mistakenly) refer to as "smudging." Smudging is a very specific method of smoke cleansing that is practiced exclusively by native American cultures, and the methods that are described here are not the same as the process of smudging. To refer to this process as smudging is insensitive, as well as inaccurate. Additionally, and as was mentioned earlier, you should be taking care not to do any sort of smoke cleansing in a room with any sensitive pets or animals who might be bothered by the smoke that you are using to cleanse a room. Most of the time, dogs and cats are okay as long as you are not exposing them to the smoke in direct ways and the room you are cleansing in this way is also ventilated, but special care should be taken with smaller pets like birds, reptiles, or rodents, as all of these animals can be extremely sensitive to pollutants in the air like smoke or other heavy particles. If you have small pets, especially birds that have very fragile respiratory systems, it is usually best to use a different form of cleansing in your home.

The next method that will be covered here is to use water for your cleansing purposes. Again, you should try to avoid using the method for things like crystals, which can become damaged or even toxic when exposed to water. However, using water can be very helpful and effective otherwise. Using water, you can try to bathe or wash an object underwater or letting it soak submerged in the water, especially running water, are all great and very effective ways of removing negative or otherwise unwanted energies. Another good method is to fill a spray bottle with water and simply mist a room or object with that water. This method can be very good for people who have small pets in the room that they are cleansing, especially birds! A lot of the birds that people keep as pets will really enjoy the light, gentle misting, and won't be hurt by the mist like they would with things like smoke. However, it is important to make sure that you won't be damaging any of the surfaces or objects that you are spraying down, like electronics. It would be a shame to have to buy a new TV because you accidentally soaked it.

Another good method is to use the earth to cleanse an object. This works best for smaller objects, as opposed to your house, of course. You might not be very happy to fill your house with sand and having to clean that up in a couple of days. However, if you bury a small object in the soil or in salt for about a day or longer, it can also remove unwanted energies. This is usually best to do by putting the salt or soil that your using in another container that will be able to hold the object that you are trying to cleanse, just to make sure that the object doesn't accidentally get lost, but as long as you can keep track of the object, it should be fine. It is usually also best to make sure that the item that you cleanse in this way either is not harmed by being surrounded by the material that you submerge it in or is easy to clean after you have retrieved it.

Light can also be somewhat effective for cleansing objects as well as charging them, depending on your intent. Most of the time, when people cleanse an object in this way, its effectiveness will be altered by the current season or the phase that the moon is in, as these factors among other relevant factors can have an impact on the kind of energy that the object will take on while it is being cleansed.

Sound can be useful for cleansing an object as well, in some cases. This method can use things like bells, drums, rainmakers, or tambourines. Using sound to cleanse an object or space can work well for larger spaces especially, and can be combined with additional actions like dancing in order to increase their effectiveness. One thing that a lot of people will do is to hang bells on their doors, which can help to shake things up and dismiss any unwanted energies when you enter a new room or space. A lot of businesses will also do this because the bells will let them know when new customers have come in, but also to help them and their customers hear the sound of the bell or chime, which can serve to "shake things up" when the customer enters this potentially new space.

Crystals can also be useful for cleansing, too. Certain crystals like citrine or smokey quartz can be very effective because they do not hold on to any specific kind of energy, so they are a sort of "objective" material that can help to dismiss unwanted energies. They also don't need to be cleansed themselves, either, which can't hurt.

Once you have finished choosing the method that you will be used to cleanse your candles or other tools, you will then want to begin to actually perform the cleansing process. It can be important to keep in mind that no matter what kind of method that you are using for the cleansing process, or what you are actually intending to cleanse, your intention is what will ultimately enable the magic to work. In order to be able to effectively use most of the methods that have been described in this chapter, you will also need to have the intention of returning your object that you are cleansing to its original, neutral state of energy. There a re a lot of ways that you can do this, but some popular methods are to visualize the energy surrounding the object changing and becoming more neutralized and to imagine the way that the new, changed energy will feel. You can also simply hold that image in your mind as you cleanse the object, and keep it in mind during the cleansing process as much as possible. As long as you have this intention with regards to the cleansing of the object or space that you are cleansing, the magic will take hold and handle the rest from there.

Once you have finished these steps, you are done! Your object should hopefully be cleansed successfully. However, if there are particularly strong energies surrounding an object, it might take a little longer for that object to "finish cooking." If this is the case, you might find that you still have not completely neutralized the energies surrounding that object or space, in which case it might be worth it to give the object another quick cleansing in order to make sure that you have finished the job.

Sometimes, a simple cleansing ritual isn't enough to completely clear particularly strong or unpleasant energy from an object or place. You might perform a cleansing on something and notice that the energy on the object is still there, or is largely unharmed or unaffected. If something still feels a little wrong, you might need to take a slightly more thorough approach for removing that energy. In this case, you will want to perform a "banishing," which is simply a stronger and more effective alternative for, especially stubborn energies. It is recommended that you do your own research about banishing and learning specific banishing spells in case you ever need to get rid of one of these difficult energies. Once you have finished a cleansing or a banishing ritual, you might want to protect the object or area from any unwanted energies in the future. Warding that object or place can be extremely helpful for this purpose, acting as a way to keep that thing safe in the future. These warding rituals can be very similar to cleansings, with the only difference being that they are a little bit more proactive than cleansings. Another good way of preventing a space or object from picking up any new unwanted energies is to charge that object or place yourself. After you've banished or cleansed the energies from something, that object will usually be devoid of its old energies, meaning that it is essentially a blank slate, ready to receive any energies that might find their way to it, even ones that you might not want around. However, if you recharge the object with your own pleasant energies, then it won't be as receptive or accepting of new energies. Effective methods for charging objects and places with particular kinds of energies will be covered in the next chapter of this book.

Chapter 5: Charging Your Candles

Once you have finished cleansing your candles, you might also want to charge them with your magical intentions. This will allow an object that you charge to be able to carry the kind of energy that you charge it with. A good place to begin with learning how to charge an object is to understand the difference between "active" and "passive" charges and how those will relate to each of your hands. Most people have two hands, one of which will normally be considered magically "active," and the other passive. The active hand is the hand that we use to send energy out with, and of course, the passive hand is the one that we typically "receive" signals through or the one that we will be able to use to sense energies with. The passive and active hands can be thought of as similar to the poles on a magnet, for this purpose. unlike a magnet, however, your hands can both be used for either purpose. In fact, many people do, and will simply use either hand or even both hands for things like charging objects or sensing their energies. This can be seen in the way that a lot of people will shake with their dominant hand, whether their primary goal in that interaction is to get a better sense of the other person's energy or to inform that person of their own. It is usually more effective to use the hand that is charged in the way that you are intending to use it, though. If you use your passive hand to get a sense of a particular object or person's energy, you will usually be able to understand that energy much more quickly, and if you use your active hand to charge objects, that will also be much more effective than if you use the passive hand.

A lot of people might assume that their dominant hand is their "active" hand and their off-hand will be the passive one, but this is not always the case. This is very common, simply because of the ways that we tend to interact with the world. If your right hand is dominant, you might use it more actively most of the time because you are more confident with that hand. But for about one-third of people, this is not the case. Some people will be much more reserved, and will typically use their dominant hand for sensing energies, or passively. It is important to be able to find out which hand will be which because you can not always rely on the instinct that your dominant hand will be the active one. There are a few ways that you can make sure which hand is which, though. One very simple method is the "handclasp" technique. If you clasp your hands together weaving your fingers between each other in an alternating pattern, your hands will usually automatically arrange themselves so that your active hand will be on the top. The hand that belongs to the thumb that rests on top of the other is typically the active one. If you try putting your hands in the opposite arrangement, your passive hand will very likely feel somewhat uncomfortable, as well. This is because that hand is much more receptive to these kinds of patterns and sensations, and you will be able to feel that this arrangement simply "feels wrong" much more easily and reliably. Another method is to simply think about how you interact with the world. Your passive hand, even if it is the more dominant one, will typically be the one that you use to feel different surfaces or objects, or to reach for things around you.

Once you understand which hand is your active hand and which is passive, you can try to get a feel for the object and its energies before you charge it yourself with your own intentions. This will be useful for letting you know if you should cleanse an object, as well, which you probably already did during the chapter on the actual act of cleansing, but it will also be useful to go over here. The best way to get a feel for objects energies is to find a calm place where you can sit down with the object in your hand. This should be your passive hand, in order to be able to get a better sense of the energies within the object, but either hand will usually work fine. You should be curling your fingers around the object, getting a feel for it and learning its surfaces and how they literally fee as well as the energies around them, without making your hand tense or too tight around the item that you are holding. You should be trying to relax and remain neutral, letting your mind be empty and ready to receive any potential energies within the object. Try to be aware of any images or thoughts that come to your mind while you are holding this object, and let them drift freely around you and disperse. You should also be looking for any literal feelings or tactile sensations that you might experience within your hands, like changes in temperature or even texture on the surface of the item, as well as any sensations that you might experience in your hands, such as numbness, tingliness, or any other unusual feelings that you might experience.

When you are finished, you can figure out whether the energies within and surrounding this item feels good to you or not. If you would like to keep those energies and build on them, then you can proceed. Otherwise, you might want to cleanse that item in order to allow it and yourself with regards to it to be able to start fresh and be clear of any negative or unusual energies. If this is the case, you might want to go back and try to cleanse the item in order to clear those energies out of it before you charge it, otherwise, you will have simply wasted your time and energy charging the item before then proceeding to cleanse if of the energy you put into it. Once you are satisfied with the state of the object before you have begun to charge it with new intentions and energies, you can move on to actually doing so.

In order to begin charging an object with new magical energies, you can hold the object in your active hand, instead of the passive one. You can also use both hands if you prefer to do it that way. You should try to experiment as much as you can in order to find out what works best for you. In the same way, as with sensing the energies of an object, you should be curling your fingers around it, gripping the object without getting too tense. Relax and let your mind be clear, allowing yourself to connect with the earth and the other elements. Then, you can try to "pull" the energy from the space around you, usually from the earth, until your own energy feels full or even overflowing. Then, you can try to visualize that energy running throughout your body, and coming up through your spine, into your arm or arms, and through the hand or hands that hold the object. You will begin to be able to feel that energy going into the object that you are charging, and the object will begin to feel different with this new energy filling and surrounding it. After a little while, your hand or hands might even begin to "tingle," and you will be able to feel the energy that is running through them. You should try to keep going, continuing to charge the object until this tingling sensation stops, and you do not feel it anymore. Once that tingling sensation has stopped, that means that the object cannot accept any more of that energy. Of course, if that object begins to feel off again or you feel like the object might need to be cleansed or refilled, you can simply repeat this procedure, cleansing it if you feel like it is necessary, and charging it again in the same way.

Chapter 6: Symbols for Your Candles

Another very useful thing for you to learn with regards to candle magic will be to understand the meanings of different symbols or sigils that you can carve into your candles as well as how and where to do so in order to achieve specific effects with your candle magic. This is a very common and popular way to strengthen the effects of candle magic and making the energy that you send off with your candle spells a little bit more specific and pointed toward a specific goal. These kinds of symbols can act as specific instructions and guides for the magical energies to follow. You might carve symbols that are representative of a specific idea or action, or a name for a person that you are sending the energy to, or even sigils to add a little bit of a stronger connection to a specific element, spirit, or other entity in order to give your candle spells a little bit of an added edge as well.

When you are carving your candles, the most important thing to have will, of course, be something to literally carve the candle with. This can be something like a knife or pen, or things that you have laying around your house like a toothpick, a nail, a safety pin, or a sewing needle. You might even use more specific objects that are representative of the intention that you have for your spell if you like, or you could just go with your fingernail. After you have found the tool that you will be using to carve your candle, you can then begin to carve your candle or candles. There are a number of different methods for carving candles for the use in candle magic, which will be listed below:

The first method here will be referred to as the "Straight Crop Method." The straight crop method is to start from the bottom of the candle and move toward the right in a straight line. If you are wanting to carve a word or a name into your candle, you would start at the bottom of the candle and carve the name or word into the candle moving toward the right, as if writing normally on a curved surface. This will have the word wrap around the candle if it is spaced properly. This method is meant to symbolize the growth of crops or other kinds of vegetation in order to bring favorable conditions. For the banishment of any possibly unfavorable conditions, you will want to start by carving from the top of your candle and move down from there in the same way, only the opposite. This will represent crops or vegetation dying off and will be useful for getting rid of those unfavorable conditions.

The next method that will be listed here is the "Stacked Letter Crop Method." The stacked letter crop method is very similar to the first method that was listed here, except that the letters will be carved on top of each other, so that they ascent vertically instead of horizontally. If you are carving a word or name, like a candle, you would start from the bottom, carving a "C," and then moving upward for the "A," "N," and so on. This should have you finish with the "E" at the top of the candle. If you want to banish an unfavorable or unpleasant condition or energy, you can reverse this process, starting instead from the top.

The third method here will be the "Spiral Crop Method." This is another very simple method to understand, and is very similar to the first two. You will want to start carving your word or name from the bottom of the candle and move to the right as well as vertically, turning the candle and moving up for each letter. Most of the time, people will move one space up and one full space to the right, so that each letter is evenly spaced. If you are writing the word candle, you might start with the C at the bottom of the candle, turning and moving it so that the A will be directly up and to the right, forming a straight line between each letter. This will create a "spiral" pattern with the letters in your "candle." This symbolizes similar concepts as the first two methods as well. In order to banish negative or unwanted energies or situations, you will reverse the process just as with the other two methods, carving your word from the top instead of the bottom.

The next method that will be listed here is referred to as the "Blessings from Heaven" method. This method is also similar to the different variations on the crop methods listed above, only done in reverse. This will be useful if you prefer to draw inspiration from the heavens and will be good for recontextualizing the banishment of unfavorable or otherwise unpleasant energies. The idea behind this method is that by carving from the top, as a reversal of the methods mentioned so far, you will be receiving a "blessing" from the heavens, which will help you to rid yourself of any unpleasant energies.

The next method that will be listed here is the "center symbol" method. This method is the simplest way to use specific sigils or other kinds of sigils with your candle spells. You can carve a sigil or other kind of symbol to represent an idea or intention for your spells or to strengthen the connection to a specific spirit, energy, or entity. A simple example of this concept is to carve a dollar sign or pound sign into the center of your candle if your intention is to draw fortune or success, or a moon to represent the goddess or the element of water.

Another good method that is useful for carving words, names, or symbols of any kind into your candles is to carve your symbol into the candle and repeat that step, by tracing over that symbol or recarving it a certain number of times. This method is typically used when a specific spell requires the caster to carve its symbol into the candle a certain number of times, so the way that you carve your symbol is less important than the actual number of times that you do so.

Another popular method that a lot of people like to use when they don't want their intentions to be discovered by other people who might find the candle that they use, especially if they prepare the candle and store it for later use is called the "spirit writing method." This method will have you use a small needle to carve into your candle. Of course, this will be able to be used with any of the other different ways to carve your words or symbols into your candles, but with a slightly different tool. You might even use a needle like this as your regular tool for carving candles. You don't have to worry about not being able to read the words or symbols that you carve into the candle, either. The "spirit" that receives your spell will be able to receive it the same way as if you wrote more visibly.

Another method that some people use is called the "bottom method." This is done by carving your words or symbols into the bottom of the candle that you will be using, instead of the side. This method can also be useful is you do not want people who find your candle to know what the candle will be used for, as most people will not look at the bottom of a candle that they find, especially if the candle is already standing up. This is a good method to use for candles that will be left burning around other people.

Chapter 7: Anointing Your Candles

Another very important thing to learn about with regards to candle magic will be anointing your candles. Charging and anointing your spell candles will help you to be able to get the most out of the specific spell or ritual that you are performing, and will make the candle and the intention that it is charged with much more potent. This action is sometimes referred to as "fixing" the candle, and there are a number of ways that you can go about doing it, depending on the specific kind of tradition that you follow.

Usually, you will want to use an oil or type of oil that is suited for magical practice, and specifically to the purpose of the spell or ritual that you are performing or aiming to perform. Some people will use olive oil or simple mundane oils for this purpose, but it is not usually recommended to do so. Things like olive oil aren't particularly well suited for magical work, and it can also feel a little bit silly to anoint your candles with cooking ingredients for some people, and this can break your immersion and connection to the spell being performed. If you want to keep a general "all-purpose" oil to use for anointing your candles and tools, you can also try things like Altar Oil, Temple Oil, Abramelin Oil, or High John the Conqueror Oil. These can be used for a lot of different purposes and can be very effective with white candles or to provide a small amount of extra help for spells performed with candles that are colored appropriately.

A lot of people will also pray over a candle before they perform a magic ritual or spell in order to charge it a little bit more or use a blessing of some sort in order to cleanse the candle before it is charged, carved and anointed. Wax is a very useful material for magical rituals, that will easily be able to absorb any kind of intentions, especially magical ones. For this reason, it is usually a good idea to purify and cleanse any candles that you obtain as quickly as possible so that they do not carry the intention of any people who have handled them in the past.

The most common method that most people will use to anoint their candles is to sit down after carving and charging the candle, and hold the candle at the base or at the middle with the passive hand, and use the active hand to anoint the candle with the oil that you are using. You will want to use your active hand to send magical intentions through the candle's top half only. You will want to rub the top half of the candle with your active hand, moving in the same direction every time. Most people will start from the middle of the candle and move upward towards the wick. You will want to repeat this process until the candle is completely covered, as well. Once this part has been completed, you will want to do the same for the bottom half of the candle, moving from the middle of the candle to the bottom until the bottom half has also been covered completely.

The reason that you will anoint one half of the candle after the other is that the two halves of your candle will represent two separate steps of the magic ritual or spell that you are performing. The first half of the candle will represent your intention being carried with the smoke up towards the heavens to be received by the "spirit," and the second half will represent that same intention or prayer being sent back down to the material world in order to be manifested. Using your hands to anoint the candle, specifically your active hand, is also representative of you acting as the agent sending specific energy out into the world to manifest as whatever goal or intent you had for your spell.

For things like banishing spells or releasing negative energies, you will usually want to anoint your candle in the opposite direction, starting with the bottom half, and then the top once that half has been completed. Additionally, there are some people who will anoint their candles starting from the outside going toward the middle, depending on the ways that they were taught. You are free to use whichever method you choose or that you find to be the most effective. Some people will even simplify the process of anointing their candles, choosing to simply anoint the candle in the direction that matches the way that they have carved their candle with whatever names, words, or symbols that they used to carve their intent into the candle, treating the anointing process as a sort of extension of the carving step. Again, though, this will depend on your particular tradition and practices, and the way that you were taught. You might even want to try experimenting in order to find out what works best, in some cases.

Additionally, while you are anointing your candles, you should try to focus your energy on the intention of your spell and the outcome that you have envisioned, in order to allow those energies and intentions to weave themselves into the candle and help to make the spell a little bit more effective and helpful. The more you stay focused on your intention, the more you will be able to specify your spell, which will ultimately help it to work in the way that you are intending for it too.

Once your candle has been anointed and you have covered your candle in the oil that you have chosen to use, you can also roll the candle in any herbs that you might have which are effective for the kind of spell that you are preparing to perform. This will help to strengthen the connection that you will be able to maintain with the deities or the elements that you will be invoking during your spell. As the candle burns, the herbs will serve a similar purpose to the oils and energies that you have anointed and charged your candle with.

Some people will sometimes use candles with glass cases, as well. These can obviously be difficult to anoint in a typical way, but there are a few methods that a lot of people will use with these glass cased candles. One is to use a nail or another kind of thin tool to make a deep hole right next to the wick of your candle, and then carefully pour or drip some of the oil that you are using into that hole in your candle. This will allow the oil to come out as the wax around the hole melts. Another method is to pour some of your oil onto the wax around the wick of your candle, forming a circle around the wick without coating it and soaking it in your oil, making it unable to ignite. Once your candle is lit, you can add more oil to the candle without harming your candle's wick. These methods will work very well for any candles with glass cases, which can be really useful for more long-term uses.

Chapter 8: Candles and Love Spells

Once you understand all of the different things that you should do in order to prepare your materials, you might want to start actually performing some real candle spells. One of the most common types of candle spells that people will start out with to learn is the "love spell." This is exactly what it sounds like. These kinds of love-based candle spells can be good for beginners and newcomers to practicing magic because they can usually be pretty easy for people to understand. Much like the concepts of love and romance themselves, love spells can sometimes be really complicated, but once you understand them and know what you want and how to go about them, they can be really straightforward as well. Additionally, love can be a very powerful feeling and even a powerful concept, which can make it much easier for you to be able to channel your goals and intentions into your candles and then into the world to be manifested and returned to you. There are a few things that you will want to remember though, that have not been discussed very deeply in this book so far when you are performing your candle spells, that can affect the ways that they function and their effectiveness. These will be listed here:

The first thing that you will need to keep in mind is to trust that your spell will do its work and have faith in that. Your magical intention is the basis of every spell that you will perform, and if you don't have faith in the spell that you perform and that it will work, then it simply won't. If you get too focused on worrying about whether your spell will work or how it will work, it can affect the way that the spell works in a negative way. Just have faith and let the spell work its magic.

While it is important to be faithful that your spell will work, it is also important that you have realistic explanations. Your love spell isn't likely to inexplicably and randomly cause a mail order bride to mistakenly wind up at your door, in the same way, that a wealth spell won't cause an ATM to fly through your window and fly open tomorrow morning. If you focus a love spell onto a specific person, you should already have a strong connection with that person in order for the spell to work, as well as a number of ethical reasons that should stop you from trying to give your childhood crush a love potion like you're a cartoon character with no regard for the consequences of their actions. You should try to manage your expectations in order to avoid disappointment when unrealistic things don't happen for no reason.

You should try not to be vague. If you are not clear about your intentions, the universe will not be able to "understand" them very well, and your spell might work in odd ways or even not at all. Your spells are simply your own energy being channeled through specific means, so to the universe, your spell will be given a sort of "telephone" effects, where if you aren't very clear about your intentions, then they will be "misunderstood," and this is bad for a number of different reasons. Try to be as specific as you can about your intentions when you cast your spells.

Another important thing to do will be to make sure that you are staying present throughout the process of executing your spell. It can be incredibly important to continue to hold your intention while your candle is burning. If you get distracted and stop focusing on your intentions while you are performing your spell, you might end up altering the way that the spell works or even cause it to not work at all. Additionally, you will be channeling your own energy and intentions through your spells, so you might feel the vibrations of those energies similarly to when you are charging your candles. You might notice those kinds of tingling sensations, and you might also be more aware of things around you like sounds, temperatures, or other kinds of changes in the environment. However, you should not be surprised or disappointed if this state of high energy or your awareness of your surroundings fades when you finish casting your spell. You won't be actively channeling that energy anymore, so you won't be as aware of those kinds of things once you're finished. You should also keep in mind that the times that it will take for spells to be realized can vary depending on a number of different factors. You might notice that some spells require a little bit more time. With these ones especially, it can be very important for you to continue to be aware and continue to look out for the effects of the spell. You should be watching for consistent patterns or events that you encounter after your spell has been cast or any shifts in your current situation with regards to the intention of your spell, especially ones that are especially unusual. Remember, also, that you will need to avoid becoming too focused on the ways that your spell will manifest. You should be trying to find a good balance between being aware and open, looking for the effects of your spell while also avoiding becoming too focused on looking for something too specific or unrealistic.

Finally, the rule of three will also be incredibly important to remember. When you cast a spell and release your energies or intentions into the world, whether those are positive or negative, they will also be sent back to you. The rule of three states that they will come back to you three times, either multiplied in intensity or frequency. This is similar to the concept of "karma." When you cast a spell or perform any kind of action, even nonmagical ones, you should remember that your actions will eventually come back to you in some form. Having the right intentions is a very important part of Wicca, and should be remembered at all times in order to help keep balance and make the world a better, healthier place for everyone.

A good spell that you can learn as a newcomer to candle magic is the love spell. This is a very simple candle spell, and the template that will be discussed here can even be repurposed to create new spells of your own design, by simply tweaking the elements of the spell that are specific to the "love spell." To perform this spell, you will first need to find your appropriate candle. For this spell, a pink candle will work best. Red candles will also do fine, but for the sake of this example, let's say it's a pink one. You will also need a few other ingredients and tools for this spell. A pen and paper to write on, a specific goal that you have with regards to your romantic interests and love, which will be discussed later, and something to light your candle with like a lighter or a match. Some other things that you might want to have with you to help make this spell just a little bit more effective are some incense. Amber, patchouli, and rose will work very well. Flowers, like pink and red roses, will be helpful but you can also include flowers that are personal to you or your love interest. A small piece of rose quartz will also be good to have around, as well as any other items that remind you of romance or love, or items that are meaningful to you and to your love interest.

Once you have gathered all of your materials, you can move on to the next part. You will want to perform this spell during a waxing or full moon. You can perform this spell at any time of day or at any point in the lunar cycle, but a waxing moon will be especially helpful for this spell. You will want to find your candle and cleanse it of any lingering energies that it might have, and then move on to carving it with whatever words, names, or symbols you might find appropriate, and anoint the candle in an appropriate oil.

Then, you will want to set up your space, placing any flowers or objects that you have collected for this spell around your altar. If you included the rose quartz that was mentioned earlier, you can also place that on the altar in front of your candle. Once you have done this, you will want to spend a few minutes in order to ground and center yourself, making sure that you have the right intention and that you are immersing yourself in that intention. You will want to invoke the deities that are relevant to those intentions and to actively visualize yourself being in a committed, loving, mutual relationship with the person you will be targeting this spell toward.

You will want to write down the goals for your romantic relationships and love that were mentioned earlier in your paper, reading it out loud as you write it down, and repeat that reading twice for a total of three times. Then you will want to place that paper under your candle, still envisioning your goals and sending their energy into your candle as you place it back above your paper. Once you have done this, you can light your candle, and say "so let it be." At this point, your candle will burn, sending your intentions out into the world, and your part is done. The spell will work its magic and take care of the rest from there.

Additionally, a lot of people from different traditions will also prefer to watch their candles after the flame has been lit in order to look for specific signs of success. To some traditions, things like the size of the flame will represent the rate or potency at which your spell is manifesting. A high, strong flame will represent a successful spell, while a lower or weaker flame will tell you that there is not a lot of spiritual energy that is being invested in your spell. Some people or groups also believe that there are signs of active opposition to your spell, which will manifest as black or especially thick smoke. This opposition could come from a number of sources such as a person involved in the spell or some unexpected factor, or even from the person who has cast the spell, in some cases. There are also other things that a lot of people will look for. Some will "read" the melted wax that might be leftover once your candle had burned out. This practice is referred to as ceromancy and is commonly practiced by people who are proficient with divinatory magic, such as scrying. The goal of ceromancy is to look for any patterns or significant shapes in the wax that might suggest a particular outcome with regards to your spell. The theory behind this is that the fire, air, or even the water represented in the wax will change the ways the wax of your candle rests in order to send you small messages about your spell. If you want, you can look for these signs when you cast your spell, but not everyone who practices candle magic believes in the validity of these signs.

You should try to avoid overthinking about these signs, however. If you lose focus, that can affect the way that your spell manifests, which can become harmful and make the messages that you see become irrelevant anyway.

Chapter 9: Candles and Money Spells

Another useful kind of candle spell that people use fairly commonly is the "money spell." This will essentially do exactly what it sounds like; provide you with a little bit of luck in boosting your finances. This is another great spell to help you to get started with candle magic, and it will also help you to find a little bit of extra luck with money, as well, which can't hurt. The trick to this spell is to try to avoid trying to figure out or predict the specific ways that this spell will be able to bring you extra money, or how this will manifest in literal terms and present itself to you. When you focus too much on how these kinds of things work, you will really only be telling the universe that you don't trust it to work these things out on your own. It's a little bit like trying to peek at your presents before Christmas. Additionally, while you're focusing on that, you might develop a sort of "tunnel vision" about it, and might stop making your own money, which will also tell the universe that you aren't willing to do some of the work yourself.

The first thing that you will need is, of course, your candle. This kind of spell will usually work best with a candle that is green or gold, to represent wealth or abundance. In addition to your candle, you will want to find some sort of vessel for the candle as you burn it, like a candle holder or a small heat-proof plate, that won't melt with the candle. Honestly, any plate that isn't made of plastic will work for this purpose. You might also want to find a cloth or a surface that you don't mind getting a little dirty during the next few steps of this spell, as well. Once you have your candle, you will probably want to cleanse it of any residual energies that it might be carrying.

After you have finished cleansing your candle, you should try to charge the candle with your intention for the spell. This can be done by holding the candle in your left hand and charging it as was described in the chapter of this book that was about charging objects. After you have finished charging your candle, you can begin carving it with a symbol that is representative of wealth or abundance. A pentagram will work fine for this purpose, but you are free to use any symbol or word that represents the concept of abundance. This symbol will be carved into the center of the body of your candle, or at the bottom, if you want to hide the fact that this candle is being used for a magic ritual.

Of course, after you have finished carving your candle, you can anoint it with your oil. Patchouli oil will work very well for this purpose, but if you don't have access to any patchouli oil, you can use olive oil or another kind of general all-purpose oil like Altar oil or temple oil to anoint your candle. Then, you will want to roll the anointed candle in a bed of dried basil, so that the basil will stick to the body of your candle. This has not been mentioned before, but the basil will also be helpful in the same way that the oil is for the purpose of this spell. Then, you will simply want to place the candle in whatever kind of vessel that you have chosen for your candle with the carved symbol facing toward yourself.

You will probably want to spend a few moments with the candle as well, grounding and centering both yourself and your candle and taking the time to conjure up the feeling of excitement and preparing yourself to receive money and wealth. You might find it helpful to imagine an exaggerated form of this wish, such as seeing yourself standing in a flowing streal of shining coins and brightly colored money or swimming in a pool of coins and gems like your favorite anthropomorphic billionaire. Once you feel connected to this image that you have visualized, you can proceed with the next step of this spell, and repeat these words:

"With this fire, I summon Nature's forces,

Money now flows to me from hidden sources."

Then you will want to light your candle. As the wick catches fire, simply say "so let it be," and let the candle burn to carry your intention away and hopefully bring you a little bit of extra income.

Chapter 10: Candles and Healing Spells

Another useful kind of candle spell that people use fairly commonly is the "healing spell." This will essentially do exactly what it sounds like; provide you with a little boost to help you or someone you know overcome an illness or other negative conditions. This is another great spell to help you to get started with candle magic, and it will also help you to to stay healthy or be healthier, or even put some positive energy out into the world for someone else, which can't hurt. The trick to these spells is to try to avoid trying to figure out or predict the specific ways that the spell will be able to heal you or make you better, or how this will manifest in literal terms and present itself to you. When you focus too much on how these kinds of things work, you will really only be telling the universe that you don't trust it to work these things out in its own ways. It's a little bit like trying to peek at your presents before Christmas.

The first thing that you will need is, of course, your candle. This kind of spell will usually work best with a candle that is white or yellow to represent health, stability, and purification. In addition to your candle, you will want to find some sort of vessel for the candle as you burn it, like a candle holder or a small heat-proof plate, that won't melt with the candle. Honestly, any plate that isn't made of plastic will work for this purpose. You might also want to find a cloth or a surface that you don't mind getting a little dirty during the next few steps of this spell, as well. Once you have your candle, you will probably want to cleanse it of any residual energies that it might be carrying.

After you have finished cleansing your candle, you should try to charge the candle with your intention for the spell. This can be done by holding the candle in your left hand and charging it as was described in the chapter of this book that was about charging objects. After you have finished charging your candle, you can begin carving it with a symbol that is representative of health or healing. An image of the sun will work fine for this purpose, but you are free to use any symbol or word that represents these concepts. This symbol will be carved into the center of the body of your candle, or at the bottom, if you want to hide the fact that this candle is being used for a magic ritual.

Of course, after you have finished carving your candle, you can anoint it with your oil. Eucalyptus or rosemary oil will work very well for this purpose, but if you don't have access to any of these, you can use olive oil or another kind of general all-purpose oil like Altar oil or temple oil to anoint your candle. Then, you will simply want to place the candle in whatever kind of vessel that you have chosen for your candle with the carved symbol facing toward yourself.

You will probably want to spend a few moments with the candle as well, grounding and centering both yourself and your candle, and taking the time to conjure up feelings related to the concepts of health or vitality. Once you feel connected to this image that you have visualized, you can proceed with the next step of this spell and repeat these words, with the blanks filled in with either "me" or the name of the person who you are intending to help heal:

"Healing light, light of love,

Fill ____ with your rays.

Renew, restore, and burn away

All illness with your blaze.

Healing fire, fire of love,

Let your flames devour

Every trace of malady-

Send ___ strength and power."

Then you will want to light your candle. As the wick catches fire, simply say "so let it be," and let the candle burn to carry your intention away and hopefully bring you or the person you are attempting to help some health and wellness.

Conclusion

Congratulations! Once you have finished reading through all of the chapters in this book and gained a complete understanding of all of the concepts and ideas that have been discussed within the book, you should have all of the tools that you need in order to understand Wiccan practices and get started with candle magic. You should have all of the tools and information that you need to begin practicing candle magic in your normal everyday life.

Learning about Wicca and beginning to learn about magic can be intimidating at first, but once you have finished this book, you should have all of the building blocks to help you move on to anything that you want to do, at least with regards to Wicca and Wiccan magic. The spells that have been explained in the last few chapters of this book can all be repurposed in ways that you find appropriate, based on the purposes and intentions that you might have at a particular time. The other parts of this book can be applied to other aspects of Wicca or magical practice as well. The first part of this book focuses primarily on the basic concepts of Wicca and different practices and traditions, which is fairly straightforward. These sections are meant to inform you and allow you to be able to form your own opinions, as well as giving you a starting point if you are not familiar with Wiccan magic practices. Then, there are a number of different aspects of candle magic that are important to learn about before you begin to actually practice magic, especially candle magic. These sections and the information that they contain can even be applied to other different kinds of magic, as well. Being able to cleanse a space or object of negative or unwanted energies will be useful outside of its use in candle magic, and the same can be said for charging an object with magical energies and applying symbols or different words to candles or other objects as well.

This book is meant to be read as an introductory guide to candle magic for complete beginners and even to Wicca in general. You will not need to have a deep understanding of Wiccan practices or the symbolism of the god and goddess or the elements in order to be able to understand the concepts and ideas that are contained within this book. All of the ideas here are related as simply as possible, so you don't need any insider knowledge in order to understand it, and any terminology that is used that might not be easily understood for the "uninitiated" will also be explained as they come up. This book is also focused on core fundamentals. Once you've finished reading it, you should have all of the tools necessary- aside from the actual tools that you will be using, of course - in order to be able to understand and master the art of candle magic and even be able to perform any spell or ritual that you might need to, by using the information here as a starting point for more complicated spells.